The Mental Health Handbook
for Primary School:
Raising Awareness of Mental Health

www.teachingexpertise.com/teachtoinspire

The Mental Health Handbook for Primary School:

Raising Awareness of Mental Health

Belinda Heaven

Author:

Belinda Heaven

Designer:

Jess Wright

Cover image: Barbara Maines

Editor:

George Robinson

Copy Editor:

Mel Maines

Illustrator:

Andrew Chubb (Andrew_Chubb@sky.com)

007-5823/Printed in the United Kingdom by CMP

Published by Speechmark Publishing Ltd., Unit C5, Sunningdale House, 43 Caldecotte Lake Drive, Caldecotte Lake Business Park, Milton Keynes, Bucks, MK7 8LF, UK

www.speechmark.net

British Library Cataloguing in Publication Data

A catalogue record for this book is available from the British Library

ISBN 978-1-906517-49-6

A CD-ROM is attached to the inside front cover and is an integral part of this publication.

Contents

Acknowledgments

I have gathered ideas from many sources such as books, from colleagues and friends. I have been fortunate to attend many conferences and gather resources to draw upon as well as my own experience.

I would particularly like to thank Poppy and all the team associated with Mental Health First Aid England. I joined the organisation three years ago and have been inspired by their enthusiasm and positive attitude towards mental health. I have taken some ideas from their activities and resources and adapted them to suit the needs of primary aged children.

I would like to thank George, my editor, who has kept me on track and for his encouragement. Also thank you to Roger for his attention to detail.

Finally a very special thank you goes to my husband, Paul, for his patience, support and love.

Forward

I am very happy to endorse this book as it makes an important contribution to a challenging area. While there are many organisations working very hard to raise awareness of mental health and mental illness, there is still a great deal of stigma and discrimination. Much of this stems from people's lack of knowledge and understanding. If you consider for a moment, when and where do people have conversations about mental health?

Mental Health First Aid England CIC, (MHFA) has some specific aims and these are outlined in this book's introduction, however, one of the most important ones is to raise awareness of mental health issues and this book contributes to that admirably. MHFA also emphasises how recovery is not only possible but likely, with the right support and care. There is a wealth of evidence to suggest that if people seek help earlier then their outcomes are much improved. Therefore, it could be argued if younger children are well informed and know they can get help then we could see a real difference in the future with potential for a reduction in enduring mental health problems. This book also encourages children and young people to learn how to take care of their own mental and emotional wellbeing as well as their physical health.

I am very pleased that MHFA has inspired some of the ideas in this book and that Belinda has adapted them for primary aged pupils. The author's idea that by talking to primary aged children about mental health will help to combat some of the stigma and increase understanding and empathy is valid. Most children and young people have a huge capacity for empathy and compassion, this is enhanced with a greater knowledge and understanding of a subject. They are like sponges and soak up information they are provided with. They also ask questions that adults would shy away from for fear of causing offence or saying the wrong thing. Mental health can be compared to bereavement, in that sense, as many people in our society feel uncomfortable talking about death. They don't even like saying the word but if you think about it the worst thing has already happened so how can you possibly make it worse?

The book provides some valuable background information for teachers as well as a PowerPoint and starter activities to engage with school staff and parents prior to delivering the lessons. Belinda has developed some engaging activities for pupils to think and talk about mental health. The lesson plans start for year 3 pupils and check out their understanding of what mental health means to them and goes on to make comparison with physical health. Pupils are asked to consider what helps and what does not in regards to health and wellbeing.

Each year group in key stage 2 has a number of lessons to choose from and the teacher can decide which is the most appropriate to suit the needs and capabilities of their pupils. The lessons stand alone or compliment the SEAL programme. They could also form part of a health focus week in school.

Poppy Jaman

Chief Executive Officer

Mental Health First Aid England CIC

Use of the CD-ROM

Many Teach to Inspire publications include CD-ROMs to support the purchaser in the delivery of the training or teaching activities. These may include any of the following file formats:

- PDFs requiring Acrobat v.3.

- Microsoft Word files.

- Microsoft PowerPoint files.

- Video clips which can be played by Windows Media Player.

- If games are included the software required is provided on the CD-ROM.

All material on the accompanying CD-ROM can be printed by the purchaser/user of the book. This includes library copies. Some of this material is also printed in the book and can be photocopied but this will restrict it to the black and white/greyscale version when there might be a colour version on the CD-ROM.

The CD-ROM itself must not be reproduced or copied in its entirety for use by others without permission from the publisher.

All material on the CD-ROM is © Heaven 2012

Website addresses are correct at the time the book is proofed for publication. Unfortunately, site owners do make frequent changes. If an address does not lead effectively to the required site we would advise you to do a search using the significant words in the www address.

Symbol Key

 This symbol indicates a page that can be photocopied from the book or printed from the PDF file on the CD-ROM. The book title appears on the page in the book but not on copies printed from the CD-ROM.

 This symbol indicates a page that can be photocopied from the book or modified and printed from the Word file on the CD-ROM. The book title appears on the page in the book but not on copies printed from the CD-ROM.

Part One

Developing Mental Health Education

Introduction

Educating children and young people about mental health and its associated problems is of vital importance. There is much stigma and discrimination in society, mainly due to a lack of understanding and ignorance. This resource will set out to challenge some of the stereotypical views and provide teachers with a comprehensive programme to enable them to deal with this important issue in a sensitive manner. Evidence of why this work should be undertaken will be highlighted throughout the programme, along with background information and signposting to additional avenues for support, advice and guidance.

Many primary schools are unsure as to how to tackle this subject and therefore choose not to. Unfortunately, while a number of national and local strategies and initiatives briefly mention mental health, the actual delivery of a specific programme such as sex and relationships (SRE) does not formally exist and also Personal, Social Health Education (PSHE) has not been made statutory by the new coalition government. Some schools will engage with outside agencies or use health professionals to tackle difficult subjects, many however, avoid them completely.

This does not mean mental health should not be discussed, in fact, quite the opposite could be argued. If society is truly going to tackle prejudice and reduce stigma and discrimination around mental ill health, then increased awareness and understanding is necessary to achieve changes in attitudes. This, in turn, will eliminate fear and ignorance thus ensuring it does not remain a 'taboo' subject. These issues are highlighted in the government paper 'No Health without Mental Health' (March 2011). This document highlights the stigma attached to mental ill health.

> No other health area combines frequency of occurrence with persistence and breadth of impact to the same extent. The stigma attached to mental health and the social barriers that surround it amplify its direct effects and damage the life chances of people with mental health problems.

(Department of Health, 2011)

There is an easy reader version available for people with learning difficulties but it could also be useful to highlight policies for children. It may be downloaded from www.dh.gov.uk/prod_consum_dh/groups/dh_digitalassets/documents/digitalasset/dh_125123.pdf. The document states that there should be equal investment for physical and mental health although it is not entirely clear about what this would look like in reality. A community interest company set up in 2010 called Mental Health First Aid England (www.mhfaengland.org) has a number of key objectives including the aim to raise awareness of mental illness in the community and also to reduce stigma and discrimination. What better place to start on this journey than with young children whose minds are open.

Children and young people have been bombarded with health messages over recent years. Most especially the 'five-a-day' campaign! There are very few primary age children who are not aware of the benefits of eating five portions of fruit and vegetables each day. Research in 2003 by Brander established that 75% of all school-aged children were dehydrated. The 'water in schools' campaign was launched with much publicity and public support. Along with these initiatives came 'wake and shake' pioneered by Ruth Mitchell in 2009 to promote physical activity in schools. The concerns over childhood obesity have gathered momentum and huge campaigns with government backing/endorsement and funding have been mounted. These include *Change for Life* and *The Health, Exercise and Nutrition in the Really Young* (HENRY programme, 2010; www.henry.org.uk).

Sadly, the same cannot be said for promoting positive mental health. It remains the poor relation and has suffered for many years through lack of awareness, and therefore, no investment. While many primary schools have a robust PSHE programme incorporating SRE, Drug Education and Healthy Eating, very few actually produce lessons specifically to discuss mental health and associated problems. Recent emphasis has been placed upon physical activity within school settings. It could be argued this is a response to concerns over childhood obesity. It would, potentially, be too late for some young people if we reached the same crisis point with mental health conditions, and with the evidence on how effective early interventions are, then to wait is foolhardy at best.

The Social and Emotional Aspects of Learning (SEAL, 2004) programme is comprehensive and well thought out. Children and young people are encouraged to develop emotional intelligence based on Daniel Goleman's (1995) principles:

- Managing feelings.

- Empathy.

- Motivation.

- Self-awareness.

- Social skills.

Each year group has a range of stories, assemblies and Circle Time activities, including small group work and materials for parents. Few teachers have accessed the staffroom activities that focus upon adult emotional intelligence, which is interesting and raises some concerns. If emotional wellbeing is to be effectively promoted in young people then surely it could be argued that wellbeing among teachers and support staff is fundamental. Corrie (2003) writes about the perceptiveness of young children and how they read body language. She goes on to quote Weatherley, 'Don't worry that your children don't listen to you, worry that they are watching everything you do'.

Many people may reflect on words from their parents and grandparents, such expressions as 'don't do as I do, do as I say' but a more modern approach is to model the sort of behaviour we would like to see in children and young people. How can teachers and support staff in schools promote self-awareness and empathy if they do not possess those themselves? SEAL is not statutory and while it teaches children and young people about emotions and feelings it stops short of discussing mental health and mental ill health. Newly qualified teachers may feel quite overwhelmed with their new role, anxious to make a good impression. They do not receive any specific training around mental health, therefore it is not surprising they do not discuss the subject for fear of saying the wrong thing. The same can be said for more experienced teachers. When you consider the high incidence of people with mental health problems and the stressful conditions of working in a school environment, it could be argued that many teachers might have mental health problems themselves and would prefer not to discuss a subject that might encroach upon their potentially fragile wellbeing.

'Mental' is a very loaded word. When questioned, both young and old render it as pathological and their expression of understanding indicates they view it with images of 'madness', people who are seriously ill, out of control and potentially dangerous.

Actually mental health is simply health of the mind. The Oxford Dictionary (11th edition revised, 2010) defines it as, 'Mental = of, in or done by the mind. Health = state of being well in body or mind.'

Exploring further with the aid of a thesaurus:

Mental:

- Cerebral.

- Intellectual.

- Deranged.

- Disturbed.

- Insane.

- Lunatic.

- Mentally ill.

- Psychiatric.

- Psychotic.

- Unbalanced and unstable.

This is without exploring derogatory language! Is it any wonder that there is so much stigma, fear and ignorance associated with Mental Health? The World Health Organisation (2001) has not amended its definition of health since 1948, and is as follows 'Health is a state of complete physical, mental and social wellbeing and not merely the absence of disease or infirmity.'

In 2008 there was a review of Child and Adolescent Mental Health Services that highlighted that unless a person is feeling mentally healthy, it is difficult for them to have optimum physical health and wellbeing. *Healthy Lives, brighter futures* (Department of Health, 2009) was a document launched jointly by the Department for Children, Schools and Families and the Department of Health. It emphasised that mental health and psychological wellbeing are fundamental to broader health and wellbeing. It also contained some useful case studies, most notably in Southampton where children and young people had been taught about mental and emotional wellbeing. The Child and Adolescent Mental Health Team at Southampton City Primary Care Trust devised a first aid course called, *Emotional First Aid for Young People*. Its aim is to teach young people how to recognise the signs of mental illness and to help them learn how to provide support and encourage the young person to seek help. More information on this interagency work may be found at (www. emotionalfirstaid.co.uk/team). When people felt able to talk about difficulties they were much more likely to seek assistance earlier and this in turn promoted better recovery. The latest government document, *No Health without Mental Health* (Department of Health, 2011), which supersedes *Brighter Futures* (2009) includes notes on the phrase 'mental health problem'. It is used as an umbrella term to describe the full range of diagnosable illnesses and disorders and it confirms the World Health Organisation's view that good or positive mental health is more than the absence or management of mental health problems, it is the foundation for wellbeing and effective functioning, both for individuals and for their communities.

Mental health may also be described as:

The strength and capacity of our minds to grow and develop, to be able to overcome difficulties and challenges and to make the most of our abilities and opportunities.

(www.youngminds.org.uk)

What do children and young people understand about mental health? When asked what mental health is, Tom aged nine said, 'It is very hard maths', although his twin sister thought it might be something to do with a healthy brain.

During health focus weeks in primary schools there is a great deal of emphasis upon physical health with many fresh fruits and vegetables being sampled and various recipes for the latest smoothies. Also, many physical activities are promoted with options to try different sports that might not be regularly on offer at school. Many do not consider mental health as part of the agenda and when the subject is raised, young children often do not know what it is. It is not until secondary school that a greater understanding becomes apparent, this perhaps is through watching soaps?

During a recent Year 10 assembly the author asked a number of questions in relation to mental health including the following:

1. **Should children and young people be taught about mental health?**

   The answer was unanimous with 100% saying 'yes it should'.

2. **When should it be taught?**

   The answers varied slightly, although following discussion, they agreed before Year 9 might be a bit frightening for pupils. They thought Year 7 pupils had too much on their minds with settling in and getting used to their new schools and that definitely primary aged children should not be taught about the problems that can occur.

3. **Who should teach it?**

   The answer was that they didn't mind as long as it was someone who knew what they were talking about, had knowledge of the subject and could talk about it in an appropriate way and explain things clearly.

4. **What did they understand about mental health?**

   The answers mainly highlighted stress, anorexia, ADHD and 'crazy people'. The pupils also commented on how the media portrayed mental health problems in a negative way, especially if celebrities were being reported upon.

Primary aged pupils are taught about the various systems in their bodies. They learn how their digestive system works, how the circulatory system works and they learn about developmental changes in sex and relationships. The emphasis on all the above is upon the physical aspects and changes, although SRE may acknowledge mood swings when talking about puberty. However, they do not learn about how their brain develops. It is helpful for young people to know that when they feel anxious or worried their brain does not function at its optimum level. The response to stress is 'flight, fight and freeze'. At this moment in time the brain functions at a very basic level, merely staying alive is the issue here. Therefore, the reptilian brain takes over, this is the most primitive part called the amygdala. Blood supply to the periphery is cut down and channelled to the vital organs. The higher cortex, where thinking, learning and understanding take place is closed down. This is because if the body is to survive it must react with lightening speed and not sit down to consider its options.

The National Society for the Prevention of Cruelty to Children (NSPCC) are the lead agency completing research and raising awareness of issues affecting children and young people's safety and development. They highlight several issues for those living with domestic abuse and experiencing neglect, emphasised by the following quote, 'Frightened children can't learn'.

Brain development takes place in the uterus and many synapses are formed following birth when attachment plays a huge part. During adolescence the brain is rewired with an opportunity for more growth in empathy and understanding. Strauch (2003) has brought together much of the research that neuroscientists are wrestling with, regarding the question, 'Why do teenagers act that way?'. With more sophisticated equipment, teenage brains are being examined to determine what exactly is going on for them during this crucial period of development. It is thought that, 'The teenage years, in fact, rival the terrible twos as a time of general brain discombobulation,' (Strauch, 2003).

The impact of mental health problems on adolescent development is far reaching. The importance of early intervention is vital for the sake of healthy development as well as the implications for whole of life functioning. Young people may resort to self-medication with drugs and alcohol as a means of coping with distressing emotions or just to block out the uncomfortable feelings. There will be associated physical health problems if this is the case. Along with poor eating habits, these may interfere with brain development in a permanent way. The negative impact may be minimised by promoting protective factors and ensuring early detection and intervention.

This resource will examine some of the protective factors contributing to mental wellbeing as well as those factors that prevent brain development and optimal functioning for the young person as a rounded, healthy human being. Risk and resilience factors play a huge part in what makes us who we are, and the lessons will explore some of the ways in which people can promote and take care of their own mental health.

Comparisons with other countries do not produce very positive findings as the Unicef Report (2007) revealed. Children and young people in the UK are reporting that they do not feel happy, compared to those in Denmark and Germany where children say they are happy and optimistic about the future. There are a number of factors that might influence this level of contentment or dissatisfaction, one of which is that children in the UK start school earlier.

> The true measure of a nation's standing is how well it attends to its children, their health and safety, their material security, their education and socialisation, and their sense of being loved, valued and included in the families and societies into which they are born.

(Unicef, 2007)

The report examined a number of dimensions to measure wellbeing including the following:

- Material wellbeing.
- Health and safety.
- Educational wellbeing.
- Family and peer relationships.
- Behaviours and risks.
- Subjective wellbeing.

While the report does not specifically examine mental health, it does pose questions that impact upon mental wellbeing, such as having someone to talk to. Sadly, the UK did not come out well when asked, 'Do you find your peers generally kind and helpful?'. More than half of the 11, 13 and 15 year olds asked were able to answer 'yes' in every OECD country except the Czech Republic and the UK.

According to the World Health Organisation:

> Being liked and accepted by peers is crucial to young people's health and development and those who are not socially integrated are far more likely to exhibit difficulties with their physical and emotional health.

(WHO, 2007)

The New Economics Foundation (NEF) was commissioned in 2008 by the UK Government to review interdisciplinary work of over 400 scientists from across the world. The aim was to identify a set of evidence-based actions to improve wellbeing, which individuals would then be encouraged to build into their daily lives. NEF proposes five ways to wellbeing:

1. Connect

Social relationships are critical to our wellbeing. Research shows that achievements associated with family and friends increases wellbeing while those associated with career, success and material gain decreases wellbeing. Building connections will support and enrich you every day.

2. Be Active

Exercise increases mood and decreases depression and anxiety. Being active also develops the motor skills in children and protects against cognitive decline in the elderly. It does not matter how you are active, as long as it is something you are able to do and enjoy.

3. Take Notice

Practising awareness of sensations, thoughts and feelings can improve both the knowledge we have about ourselves and our wellbeing. Learning to savour the moment and becoming more aware of the world around you will help you to appreciate what matters to you. It is also useful to reflect upon this.

4. Keep Learning

Learning encourages social interaction and increases self-esteem and feelings of competency. Trying something new or rediscovering an old interest, taking on some more responsibility can build confidence and can also be fun.

5. Give

Cooperative behaviour activates reward areas of the brain, suggesting we are hard wired to enjoy helping others. Seeing yourself and your happiness linked to the wider community can be incredibly rewarding and creates connections with the people around you.

The graph below illustrates that since 1973, while the gross domestic product has increased hugely, indicating we all have many more material possessions, the level of satisfaction has not!

(New Economics Foundation, 2004)

In 2004, NEF completed a study into wellbeing in young people in Nottingham. Their report identified how secondary school-aged children become bored, stop learning and no longer enjoy the activities available at school. A two dimensional model of wellbeing was adopted:

1. Life satisfaction captures pleasure, enjoyment and contentment.

2. Personal development captures curiosity, enthusiasm, absorption, flow, exploration, commitment, creative challenge and also potentially, meaningfulness.

This builds upon the work of Seligman (1998) who launched Positive Psychology as an official area of study. Over the past decade there has been increased interest in happiness and it is now taken much more seriously. Teaching happiness helps children and young people to become well-rounded individuals and achieve their greatest potential (www. authentichappiness.org).

Why it is Important

How are young people to learn about mental health if nobody talks to them about it? All they will learn is that it is not to be mentioned. This perpetuates the myth that it is dangerous and to be avoided. An organisation called Mindful Employer (www.mindfulemployer.net/charter.html) established in 2004, has identified how people choose not to reveal that they have had mental health problems when applying for jobs. Its mission is to promote positive attitudes to mental health problems in the workplace. It recognises how people with mental health problems have been discriminated against. It quotes the Equality Act of 2010 in the charter for employers who are positive about mental health as detailed below and available to download from their website.

As an employer we recognise that:

- people who have mental health issues may have experienced discrimination in recruitment and selection procedures. This may discourage them from seeking employment

- while some people will acknowledge their experience of mental health issues in a frank and open way, others fear the stigma will jeopardise their chances of getting a job

- given appropriate support, the vast majority of people who have experienced mental ill health continue to work successfully, as do many with ongoing issues.

As an employer we aim to:

- show a positive and enabling attitude to employees and job applicants with mental health issues. This will include positive statements in local recruitment literature

- ensure that all staff involved in recruitment and selection are briefed on mental health issues and The Equality Act 2010, and given appropriate interview skills

- make it clear in any recruitment or occupational health check that people who have experienced mental health issues will not be discriminated against, and that disclosure of a mental health problem will enable both employee and employer to assess and provide the right level of support or adjustment

- not make assumptions that a person with a mental health problem will be more vulnerable to workplace stress or take more time off than any other employee or job applicant

- provide non-judgemental and proactive support to individual staff who experience mental health issues

- ensure all line managers have information and training about managing mental health in the workplace.

Everyone acknowledges physical health, you can see it. For example, a broken leg is placed in a plaster cast to allow it time to heal and inhalers are taken for relief of asthma. We can't see inside people's minds and therefore do not appreciate when they are troubled or distressed.

Physical pain may be observed, as a person may appear sweaty, body language and facial expression would also reveal something of the nature of the pain. This is not always the case with mental health and many individuals become expert in hiding their true feelings or how disturbed they are. It is worth considering some fine comedians including Stephen Fry and Ruby Wax who have both battled with mental health problems their entire lives and often appear perfectly fine, presenting a jolly public persona. They are part of what is referred to as England's most ambitious campaign to end discrimination faced by people with mental health problems (www.time-to-change.org.uk).

If young people are taught about emotions, thoughts, feelings and moods with an emphasis on what 'normal' development looks like, then it naturally follows that discussion on what can go wrong could or even should take place. There is evidence to suggest that early intervention prevents worsening of mental health problems. The Early Psychosis Declaration (EPD) is an International Consensus Statement about early intervention and recovery for young people, jointly issued by The World Health Organisation and the International Early Psychosis Association (2004). The document describes a number of five-year measurable outcomes that an individual and their family can expect from services that have successfully implemented a comprehensive and effective programme, and can be downloaded at www.rethink.org/about_mental_illness/early_intervention/ support_for_family_and_carers/the_early.html.

It contains vision and values as follows:

- Challenge stigmatising and discriminatory attitudes so that young people are not disadvantaged by their experiences and are truly included in their local communities.

- Generate optimism and expectations of positive outcomes and recovery so that all young people with psychosis and their families achieve ordinary lives.

- Raise wider societal awareness about psychosis and the importance of early intervention.

- Attract and encourage practitioners from a wide range of health, social, non-governmental agencies (for example, charitable, voluntary and youth), education and employment services to reflect on how they can better contribute to supporting young people with psychosis, their families and friends.

- Respect of the right of recovery and social inclusion to support the importance of personal, social, educational and employment outcomes.

- Respect of the strengths and qualities of young people with a psychosis, their families and communities, encouraging ordinary lives and expectations.

- Services that actively partner young people, their families and friends to place them at the centre of care and service delivery, at the same time sensitive to age phase of illness, gender, sexuality and cultural background.

- Use of cost effective interventions.

- Respect of the right for family and friends to participate and feel fully involved.

This is backed up by a National Health Service Publication (2011) entitled *Improved Access To Psychological Therapies* (IAPT) (http://www.iapt.nhs.uk/). It has been accompanied by a review of Child and Adolescent Mental Health Services. If emerging problems could be identified more readily and support accessed sooner, many more serious problems could be prevented and ultimately treated effectively. The National Service Framework, Department of Health (2004) stated that:

> Untreated mental health problems create distress not only in the children and young people, but for their families and carers, continuing into adult life and affecting the next generation.

A key message throughout this resource is that recovery is not only possible but most likely. According to *No Health without Mental Health* (Department of Health, 2011) the term 'recovery' has developed a specific meaning in mental health that is not the same as, although it is related to 'clinical recovery'. It has been defined as:

> A deeply personal, unique process of changing one's attitudes, values, feelings, goals, skills and/or roles. It is a way of living a satisfying, hopeful and contributing life, even with limitations caused by the illness. Recovery involves the development of new meaning and purpose in one's life.

(Mental Health First Aid England, 2010)

Mental Health First Aid England (MHFA, 2010) also emphasises that recovery from mental ill health is not only possible but likely. A MHFA course will teach you to:

- spot the early signs of a mental health problem

- feel confident helping someone experiencing a problem

- provide help on a first aid basis

- help prevent someone hurting themselves or others

- help stop a mental illness from getting worse

- help someone recover faster

- guide someone towards the right support

- reduce the stigma of mental health problems.

MHFA state recovery is about much more that the absence of symptoms. For some people it can be a long-term process, often described as a journey and it may not necessarily be a linear process. Recovery is a deeply personal process but research shows that a positive attitude and expectation of recovery will improve the outcome.

There are many myths and misunderstandings associated with mental ill health, one of which is that once an individual has become mentally unwell they are never fully recovered and will always have a tendency to become unwell probably under very minimal pressure.

It is helpful to revise our own definition of what recovery means and The Mental Health Foundation (2011) www.mentalhealth.org.uk/ highlight a number of aspects relating to this important area. They are the UK's leading mental health research, policy service improvement charity and they refer to a process that:

- provides a holistic view of mental illness that focuses on the person, not just their symptoms
- believes recovery from severe mental illness is possible
- is a journey rather than a destination
- does not necessarily mean getting back to where you were before
- happens in 'fits and starts' and, like life, has many ups and downs
- calls for optimism and commitment from all concerned
- is profoundly influenced by people's expectations and attitudes
- requires a well organised system of support from family, friends or professionals
- requires services to embrace new and innovative ways of working.

They also identify many of the factors that contribute to recovery from their extensive research that include:

- good relationships
- financial security
- satisfying work
- personal growth
- the right living environment
- developing one's own cultural or spiritual perspectives
- developing resilience to possible adversity or stress in the future.

Further factors highlighted by people as supporting them on their recovery journey include:

- being believed in
- being listened to and understood
- getting explanations for problems or experiences
- the opportunity to temporarily resign responsibility during periods of crisis.

People living in poverty not only lack financial resources to maintain basic living standards but also have fewer educational and employment opportunities, are exposed to adverse living environments and are less able to access good quality health care. These factors put them at a higher risk of developing a mental disorder. When people develop mental disorders they are likely to descend further into poverty, both because of increased health care costs as well as decreased productivity and lost opportunities for employment.

(WHO, 2001)

National Initiatives

Educating children and young people about mental health is vitally important. It is highlighted in a number of government documents and initiatives. While the coalition government has not actually stated that the *Every Child Matters'* agenda no longer exists, they are referring to it as helping children to achieve more. Paul Ennals, who was partly responsible for the development of ECM and is the Chief Executive Officer from the National Children's Bureau, suggests that the way forward is to drop the brand or label but insists the importance of the outcomes remain (www.cypnow.co.uk/Joint_working/article/1060947/Every-Child-Matters-defunct/).

There are a number of government documents that support the development of this programme. They are listed below with a summary of the content and a link is provided should more details be required.

No Health without Mental Health: A Cross-Government Mental Health Outcomes Strategy for People of all Ages (2011)

(www.dh.gov.uk/en/publicationsandstatistics/publications/publicationspolicyandguidance/DH_123991)

There are six shared objectives that underpin the framework:

1. More people will have good mental health by starting well, developing well, working well, living well and ageing well.

2. More people with mental health problems will recover.

3. More people with mental health problems will have good physical health.

4. More people will have positive experiences of care and support.

5. Fewer people will suffer avoidable harm.

6. Fewer people will experience stigma and discrimination by increasing public understanding.

The mental health of children and young people is to be made a key part of the strategy with money being channelled into early intervention, including talking therapies for young people.

Targeted Mental Health in Schools Programme (2008-2011)

(www.education.gov.uk/publications/standard/Pupilsupportwelfareandbehaviour/Page3/DCSF-00784-2008)

Local authorities were invited to bid for government funding to tackle mental health problems in schools. The initiative was to be jointly led by representatives from health and education and each local authority could pilot their own programme.

A large number provided training in schools to highlight the importance of understanding mental health problems. Many, recruited primary mental health workers to be based in schools to provide support, advice and guidance to teachers and school support staff who are dealing with the issues faced by pupils on a regular basis. Findings and outcomes may be viewed on the link above. Feedback from the Gloucestershire project that worked with 24 schools over the three-year period included:

It is easier to pick up with younger children how they are feeling, they will be more obviously upset and more openly express how they are feeling than the older children.

Most of the staff took on board what the project was trying to achieve, some are less keen. You always get some people who see children as being naughty rather than they might be having some real difficulties.

It generated lots of new ideas and we looked at what we already have in place in school. Staff found it interesting to reflect on their own behaviour and how they came together to work through issues.

(Office for Public Management, 2010)

The schools were assured of their anonymity while providing feedback.

Healthy Schools Plus/Enhancement Model (2009)

(www.surreyhealthyschools.co.uk/downloads/Healthy_Schools_Plus_Enhanced_Status_pack_2008.pdf)

The Healthy Schools Enhancement Model has been designed to help schools to develop the wider thinking and planning they will need to do to achieve better outcomes around health and wellbeing for children and young people. It has also been designed to help schools to strive to achieve behaviour changes for lasting health and wellbeing in children and young people, with a particular focus on providing targeted support for those who are most at risk. Schools will work closely with key partners towards achieving locally agreed health and wellbeing outcomes. This will reflect school-based local and national priorities as outlined in the Local Area Agreements, Children and Young People's Plans and Primary Care Trust operational plans. The enhancement model will provide schools with rigorous health and wellbeing evidence for school improvements plans, the Ofsted self-evaluation form (SEF) and the pupil level wellbeing indicators and school report card. It will provide vital leadership in translating into practice the Government's vision of the 21st Century School and helping to make this the best country in the world to grow up.

New Ofsted Framework (2009)

(www.ofsted.gov.uk/Ofsted-home/Publications-and-research/Browse-all-by/Documents-by-type/Consultations/Indicators-of-a-schools-contribution-to-wellbeing)

The wellbeing indicators include:

- How effective, efficient and inclusive is the provision of education, integrated care and extended services in meeting the needs of learners?
- How good is the overall personal development and wellbeing of the learners?
- The extent of learners' spiritual, moral, social and cultural development.
- The extent to which learners adopt healthy lifestyles.
- The extent to which learners adopt safe practices.
- How well learners enjoy their education.
- The attendance of learners.
- The behaviour of learners.
- The extent to which learners make a positive contribution to the community.
- How well learners develop workplace and other skills that will contribute to their future economic wellbeing.

The Children's Plan (2007)

(www.dcsf.gov.uk/publications/childrensplan)

This builds upon the *Every Child Matters'* agenda. The government acknowledged that sometimes parents need help and support bringing up children. It also identified that good health is vital if children and young people are to enjoy their childhood and achieve their full potential. If good habits are established in childhood, this will provide the basis for lifelong health and wellbeing. The government stated that in order to improve children's health they would do the following:

- Publish a Child Health Strategy in Spring 2008, produced jointly between the Department for Children, Schools and Families and the Department of Health.

- Review Child and Adolescent Mental Health Services to see how universal, mainstream and specialist support services can be improved for the growing number of children and young people with mental health needs.

This initiative was born out of a realisation by the government that mental health problems among children and young people were increasing. Therefore, it allocated funding to address this issue and invited local authorities to join with NHS Primary Care Trusts to bid for funding with proposed plans to tackle the issues. The vision was for change to make England the best place in the world for children and young people to grow up in by 2020. There was an interim report in 2008 which may be found on the website.

National Service Framework (NSF) for Children, Young People and Maternity Services (2004) Department of Health

(www.dh.gov.uk/policyandguidance/healthandsocialcaretopics/childrenservices)

The NSF establishes clear standards for promoting the health and wellbeing of children and young people and for providing high quality services that meet their needs. Standard 9 specifically focuses upon the mental health and psychological wellbeing of children and young people and states that:

> All children and young people, from birth to their eighteenth birthday, who have mental health problems and disorders have access to timely, integrated, high quality multidisciplinary mental health services to ensure effective assessment, treatment and support for them and their families.

The document also states that all staff working directly with children and young people should have sufficient knowledge, training and support to promote psychological wellbeing of children, young people and their families.

Every Child Matters (2004) Department for Children, Schools and Families

(www.everychildmatters.gov.uk/publications)

This focuses upon five outcomes:

1. Being Healthy – this means both physically and mentally.

2. Staying Safe – to ensure that children and young people feel safe. Consideration must be given to the issues that could prevent that, including domestic abuse, bullying and family break up as these all impact upon mental health.

3. Enjoying and Achieving – this is not going to be possible when mental health problems prevail.

4. Making a Positive Contribution – unless the other outcomes are in place children and young people are not going to be able to achieve this. The New Economics Foundation (2004) researched the importance of giving, and highlights the importance of this outcome.

5. Economic Wellbeing – there are strong links between poverty and mental health problems.

Choosing Health (2004) Department of Health

(www.dh.gov.uk/publications)

This document focuses upon a number of health inequalities and takes a holistic approach to health. Specifically improving mental health is highlighted within the executive summary:

> …because mental wellbeing is crucial to good physical health and making healthy choices, because stress is the most common reported cause of sickness absence and a major cause of incapacity, and because mental ill-health can lead to suicide.

National Institute for Health and Clinical Excellence (NICE, 2006)

(www.nice.org.uk/nicemedia/live/11948/40119/40119.pdf)

NICE were asked by the Department of Health to develop guidance on school-based interventions aimed at promoting good mental health among children aged 11 and under. It provided recommendations for good practice based on the best evidence available and was aimed at teachers, governors and support staff in schools. In 2008 more guidance was issued on social and emotional wellbeing in schools.

Children and Young People's Mental Health Coalition (CYPMHC, 2010)

(www.cypmhc.org.uk/resources/improving_children_and_young_peoples_mental_health/)

This organisation brings together leading mental health charities to campaign with and on behalf of children and young people in relation to their mental and emotional wellbeing. The aim of CYPMHC is to achieve policy changes at the highest level that will directly improve the mental and emotional wellbeing of children and young people across the UK.

The four key areas for CYPMHC are:

1. The Early Years – to have greater emphasis on the psychological aspects of parenting and providing parents/care givers with the knowledge and tools to improve their own and their children's mental health and wellbeing.

2. Building Emotional Resilience – to support all children and young people to meet the challenges of growing up by equipping them with self-awareness and emotional resilience to achieve good mental health.

3. Reaching Adulthood – to achieve greater recognition that development to adulthood continues to the mid-20s and demands a responsive and flexible approach across all areas of health and social policy and practice.

4. Seldom Heard Voices – to give all children and young people timely access to good quality mental health and wellbeing support, with effective outcomes, regardless of the ethnicity, gender, sexual preference, disability or other personal experiences.

Facts and Figures

An important reason for the development of this resource is that mental health problems are very common.

- In 2004 around 10% of 10-16 year olds had a diagnosable mental health disorder (Department of Health, 2004).

- 50% of young adults with mental health disorders had a diagnosis by the age of 15 and nearly 75% by their late teens (Mental Health Policy Group, 2006).

- For those aged 15-24 suicide is the most common cause of death (Adelstein and Mardon, 2010).

- 54% of young offenders have suffered a significant bereavement within two years of first offending (DfE, 2003).

- In 2005 the cost of mental health problems was greater than that of crime and all monies spent on the NHS and social services in the UK (HM Treasury, 2005).

- By 2020 depression will be the second leading contributor to the global burden of disease (WHO, 2001).

There has been a significant increase in the number of young people self-harming in the last decade and rates in the UK are among the highest in Europe (Samaritans, 2010). Childline have reported a 30% increase and 91% were girls. Self-harm, as with many other mental health issues, is largely misunderstood and many people believe it is always linked with suicide. This is not the case for many young people who describe it as a way of coping, so therefore more about staying alive rather than a wish to end their life. The rate of self-harm is relatively low in early childhood but increases rapidly with the onset of adolescence (Hawton, 2003).

It is behaviour not an illness and should always be taken seriously. It can take many forms and varies in severity with each individual. There is a higher incidence among minority groups including gay, lesbian and bisexuals discriminated against by society (Meltzer et al., 2002). There is also evidence to suggest that it is affecting much younger children. A study by Nicholls (2011) discovered a shocking 208 cases of early onset eating disorders among the under 13s. There are many reasons why young people do not get help with mental health problems including the following:

- I prefer to manage the problem myself.

- I don't believe anything can help.

- I don't know where to get help.

- I am worried about what others will think.

(The Child and Adolescent Component of the National Survey of Mental Health and Wellbeing, 1998)

Gloucestershire's Health and Wellbeing Team completed an online pupil survey with nearly 20,000 pupils aged between 8 and 15 years. This was the third in a series of surveys completed every two years, which started in 2006. It revealed that many young people have thought about harming themselves and feel very stressed. When questioned about what they wanted they said more information, guidance and support. Stress came out as the top answer along with some body image issues for Year 6 girls. While many said they felt optimistic about the future, a significant number said they did not and felt unhappy quite a lot of the time, with nobody to talk to about their worries. This clearly highlights much angst among young people. Also, that there is little point in asking such questions if we are not going to act upon the answers.

How to Use this Programme

This mental health and emotional wellbeing education resource has been designed to be user-friendly and allow teaching staff to deliver effective lessons for Key Stage 2 pupils.

There is no statutory obligation to deliver lessons on mental health so the lessons mainly stand alone, although they may compliment some SEAL materials the school are already using. They could also form part of a special project or health focus week. The following areas will be covered:

- Exploration of what mental health is and what it is not, including stigma and discrimination.

- Mental ill health and what can go wrong as well as normal brain development.

- What helps and what does not. Risk and resilience factors.

- Mental health promotion and why it is important.

Each lesson plan considers the requirements of the teacher with notes and activities. The activity pages can be copied from the book or printed from the CD-ROM.

The introduction emphasises the importance of mental health education for primary schools. It highlights the rates of mental ill health among children and young people including figures relating to self-harm and suicide. There are additional facts in the PowerPoint for teachers and at the start of each set of lessons there are hints on how to introduce the topic.

It is interesting to note that for 'sex and relationships' education every school is required to have a policy. Indeed for many subject areas, schools are required to have policies. For mental health this is not the case. The PowerPoint presentation gives some suggestions on how the subject of mental health might be included in existing policies, also how a programme of work might gain greater recognition and support by involving senior leadership in the school. There is much evidence to suggest that this creates more commitment and strengthens the delivery of topic areas (OPM, 2010).

Working with parents/carers and families is vital for complete engagement with the programme and the delivery as a partnership between home and school will enhance the learning immeasurably. Many of the activities designed for use with the pupils may be adapted for use with parents/carers and staff at school.

The lesson plans suggested are for certain age groups, however, it is dependent upon the ability and maturity of the group. The teacher is the best person to determine which sections are used with their current class and also how long they might spend on each activity.

The resource is very flexible and the lessons may be used as a stand-alone part of the curriculum. Alternatively, some schools have a health focus week and it might be more suitable for the lessons to be delivered as part of a whole 'healthy body, healthy minds' topic. Another suggestion might be if the school is focusing upon anti-bullying week and using the SEAL materials, it would be useful to consider the impact of bullying on a young person's emotional and mental health. The most important factor is that children and young people receive some very accurate information about mental health.

The programme is aiming to raise awareness and create better understanding of mental health, which in turn challenges stigma, prejudice and discrimination. It would be most useful if the staff in school could receive training sessions and explore some of their own understanding of mental health along with values, attitudes and experiences. This is where the PowerPoint presentation in conjunction with some staff activities could help to launch the programme. It would be good to build staff confidence and ensure clear consistent messages were being delivered to the children. Any programme, if it is to be effective, needs the support of the senior management team as well as governors and parents/carers. That way the pupils benefit from a conjoined approach to the subject and receive some consistent messages in a comprehensive way.

When lessons are delivered, questions from children will inevitably arise. The resource will offer suggestions as to how to deal with potentially difficult questions and provide examples of the sort of issues that children might raise. Examples of the type of questions are provided. Also, there is a directory that contains a list of books that teachers and parents could read and a list of websites and helplines for additional support, advice and guidance.

A new organisation called Mental Health First Aid England promotes the discussion of issues such as suicide. Clearly this will raise concerns for some members of staff, especially if this is something that has affected them personally. Therefore, it is suggested the resource is handled with care. If, for example, a member of staff has experienced some mental health problems themselves, they might feel comfortable sharing their views and experiences. Alternatively, some may not wish to disclose any information about themselves or their families at all. The most important aspect of this is that the person delivering the lesson is comfortable with the material and potential questions that may arise. Young people are incredibly perceptive and know if they are not being given the whole picture and ultimately mixed messages may be conveyed which will add to their confusion.

This resource aims to include everything that primary schools need to deliver an education programme on mental and emotional wellbeing at Key Stage 2. Young people deserve to learn about this very important aspect of their lives.

Child Protection and Safeguarding

When delivering this programme on mental health, issues may be raised that cause concern. For example, when discussing what might impact in a negative way upon mental health, a child may reveal that they are exposed to, or experiencing, domestic abuse or bullying. As with any aspect of school life the child protection policy must be adhered to and procedures followed. If additional support or guidance is required the school may contact their local safeguarding board.

Confidentiality

If a child reveals an issue for concern to the member of staff delivering the lesson, they should listen to what the child tells them, but under no circumstances guarantee confidentiality, as it might be the child is at risk and procedures should be followed without deviation. Protection of the child is paramount at all times.

Working Together Agreement

Due to the nature of the material within the lessons it is suggested that a 'Working Together Agreement' is created before the programme is delivered. This agreement protects teaching staff and also provides boundaries, therefore creating a safe environment. It consists of a list of ideas that pupils and staff would like to adhere to while in the mental health and emotional wellbeing sessions. The list should be displayed where everyone can see it and throughout the lessons, as you may need to refer to it at any time. It would be beneficial to keep parents and carers informed of this agreement and you could involve them in the development of it.

A few examples of what might be included in your own Working Together Agreement:

- Respect others' views.
- No laughing at others' questions.
- Take responsibility for your own actions and contributions.
- Use 'I' language and speak for yourself.
- Share the story, not the person to ensure confidentiality.
- No personal comments and judgements.
- Ask questions.
- The right to remain silent.
- Keep a sense of perspective.
- Challenge discrimination in a constructive manner.

A useful suggestion is to have a question box. This enables people to put a question in the box ready for discussion within the next session.

The teacher can check them out and it really helps to tailor the lesson to meet the needs of the children and young people when asking them what 'they' need to know.

Many schools have working together agreements that are circulated to parents/carers. An emphasis on working together in partnership is always helpful to promote good communication and understanding. For this reason, there are some tips on the following pages regarding engagement with parents and some suggestions about how to organise a parents' evening to inform them of your intentions to run the programme. It also provides an opportunity to discuss their concerns and increase their own knowledge and understanding of mental and emotional wellbeing.

Working with Parents/Carers

> Parents are the key to achieving the best physical and mental health and wellbeing outcomes for their children.

(Department of Health, 2009)

Many parents will not have talked to their children about mental health and they may even resent the school tackling this subject. Feedback from a primary school taking part in the targeted mental health project led by the government, revealed that parents did not like the use of the word 'mental' and in order to engage with them the local project was renamed 'Healthy Minds Matter'. Conversely, some parents will be more than happy to let the schools take responsibility for talking to their children about mental health. One school in the project reported that:

> You might get a mum saying the daughter has mental health problems, but actually it is the mother herself.

(OPM, 2010)

Unfortunately most people have a negative view of mental health and regard it as an unpleasant subject that makes them feel uncomfortable. This stems from ignorance and a lack of understanding. They probably have never had this sort of conversation themselves and would prefer not to. This, in itself, leads to further stigma, prejudice and discrimination. Parents will need reassurance that the subject is being delivered and discussed in a thoughtful, considerate manner. They may wish to view the materials before their children receive them.

Throughout the programme from Year 3 to Year 6 there are a number of lessons within the themes to challenge stigma and discrimination. These include:

- Year 3, Theme Two, Lesson 2, Healthy Minds and Healthy Brains activity.

- Year 4, Theme Two, Lesson 2, Language of Mental Health activity.

- Year 5, Theme One, Lesson 2, Myth or Reality activity.

- Year 6, Theme One, Lesson 2, Mental Health and the Media activity.

A suggestion here is for the school to invite parents and carers, as well as governors, to an informal meeting where the lesson plans may be shared and an opportunity for questions given. The resource includes a template letter that may be adapted. Parents can be provided with additional resources so that they feel able to answer questions asked at home, following the lessons. Some of the activities planned for use with the pupils could be used with the parents, for example, the quiz for Year 5 pupils in Theme Three, Lesson 1, to determine knowledge and understanding will also promote useful discussion.

Mental Health First Aid England highlights that talking about subjects such as suicide will not provide young people with suggestions that they would not already have thought of. They go further:

> Contrary to common belief, there is evidence that direct questioning does not encourage a person to pursue suicidal behaviour. It signals to them that you care, that you are concerned and have a genuine desire to be helpful. It also signals that you are a person who is willing and able to talk about suicide.

(MHFA, 2010)

Some parents may welcome an opportunity to learn more about mental health problems themselves and appreciate their children gaining knowledge and life skills in the sessions. Suffice to say, parents vary enormously, as do their children. While some will not wish to discuss or reveal any information, some may take the opportunity to share experiences that could make others uncomfortable. It will be dependent upon the teacher leading the session to manage these issues.

As with many other topic areas there are key elements to successfully working with parents and carers:

- The full support and engagement of the headteacher and senior leadership team is an important requirement.

- Care should be taken not to make judgements and stereotype parents.

- Parents and carers should be kept well-informed.

- An open relationship should be maintained between school and home.

Communication is the key ingredient here and a letter outlining what will be covered in the lessons can be found at the end of the chapter. There is a book list at the back of the resource that may be printed for parents, as well as a list of organisations.

Outline of the Parents Meeting

The following points should be considered and included for the parents' meeting and may be adapted for different settings:

- Welcome and introductions.

- Establishment of ground rules.

- Exploration of understanding of mental health.

- Explanation of why talking about mental health is important using background information and quotes from the programme.

- Ensure parents and carers know that the programme is evidence-based and well-researched, not just a good idea that somebody thought of in a random way.

- Show materials from the pack and encourage parents to try the quiz or take part in another activity from the programme, so that they understand what their children will be considering and have empathy.

- Highlight the issues around stigma and discrimination.

- Show evidence of how early interventions are effective.

- Explain why children do not ask for help when they are struggling.

- Ask about modelling behaviour.

- Allow lots of time for questions.

A useful quote from the programme could be included:

> Two key skills are necessary for positive mental health, learning to cope and even prosper in the face of adversity and the ability to create feelings of happiness through healthy, positive means. If children and young people have pleasure, engagement and meaning in life, they are likely to experience happiness, life satisfaction, wellbeing and lead more flourishing lives.

(Ward, 2008)

Questions Children Ask

Can children have mental health problems?

Yes, an increasing number of young people are suffering with mental health problems although many of them are not diagnosed or detected until much later.

Why do some people suffer from depression and others don't?

Depression is not a choice and it may affect any one of us at any time. Some people are more susceptible to mental health problems than others and there are many factors that influence its development.

Are people who become depressed just really lazy and weak?

No, depression has nothing to do with being lazy or weak. Often it is to do with the chemistry in the brain being altered.

Are people with mental health problems below average intelligence?

Mental health problems are not linked to a person's intelligence.

Can you get better if you have a mental health problem?

Yes, absolutely, many people who have experienced and suffered with mental ill health have gone on to enjoy happy, fulfilling lives and have made a full recovery, in fact recovery is more likely than long-term problems persisting.

Are mental health problems common?

Yes they are, and most of us will experience some form of mental health problem at some stage in our lives. Often it is a depression or anxiety associated with a life event such as bereavement.

Why do people self-harm?

Many people who self-harm describe it as a coping strategy and it is not necessarily an indication that somebody wants to end their life. It does show that they are experiencing some emotional distress and may need help and support.

What is schizophrenia?

There are many misunderstandings about schizophrenia. It is not a split personality or a shattered one. It describes an episode where the individual might be seeing things that are not there or hearing voices and their sense of reality is altered. This might present as paranoia, which is where a person thinks everyone is out to get them.

Are people with mental health problems dangerous?

Only a very few, most are more at risk of harming themselves than others.

If your parents have a mental health problem will you inherit it?

Not necessarily, you can't 'catch' a mental health problem but if someone in your family suffers then it will impact upon everybody around them and they may need support and care.

Example of a Letter to Parents/Carers

Dear Parent/Carer

As part of our Personal, Social and Health Education programme some of our teachers and local health professionals have recently started to work together to plan a Mental Health and Emotional Wellbeing Education Programme for pupils. We have had many health focus weeks promoting healthy eating and exercise for healthy bodies, we are now going to focus upon healthy minds.

The programme will include lessons about the following:

- Promoting greater understanding of mental health, including stigma, prejudice and discrimination.
- What can go wrong when people become mentally unwell.
- What helps and what does not.
- Risk and resilience factors affecting mental health.
- How to promote positive mental health and why it is important.

We plan to start this work on: ....

If you would like to find out more about this programme and have an opportunity to view the lesson plans we intend to use, we welcome you to an informal meeting in an after school session on:

....

Yours sincerely

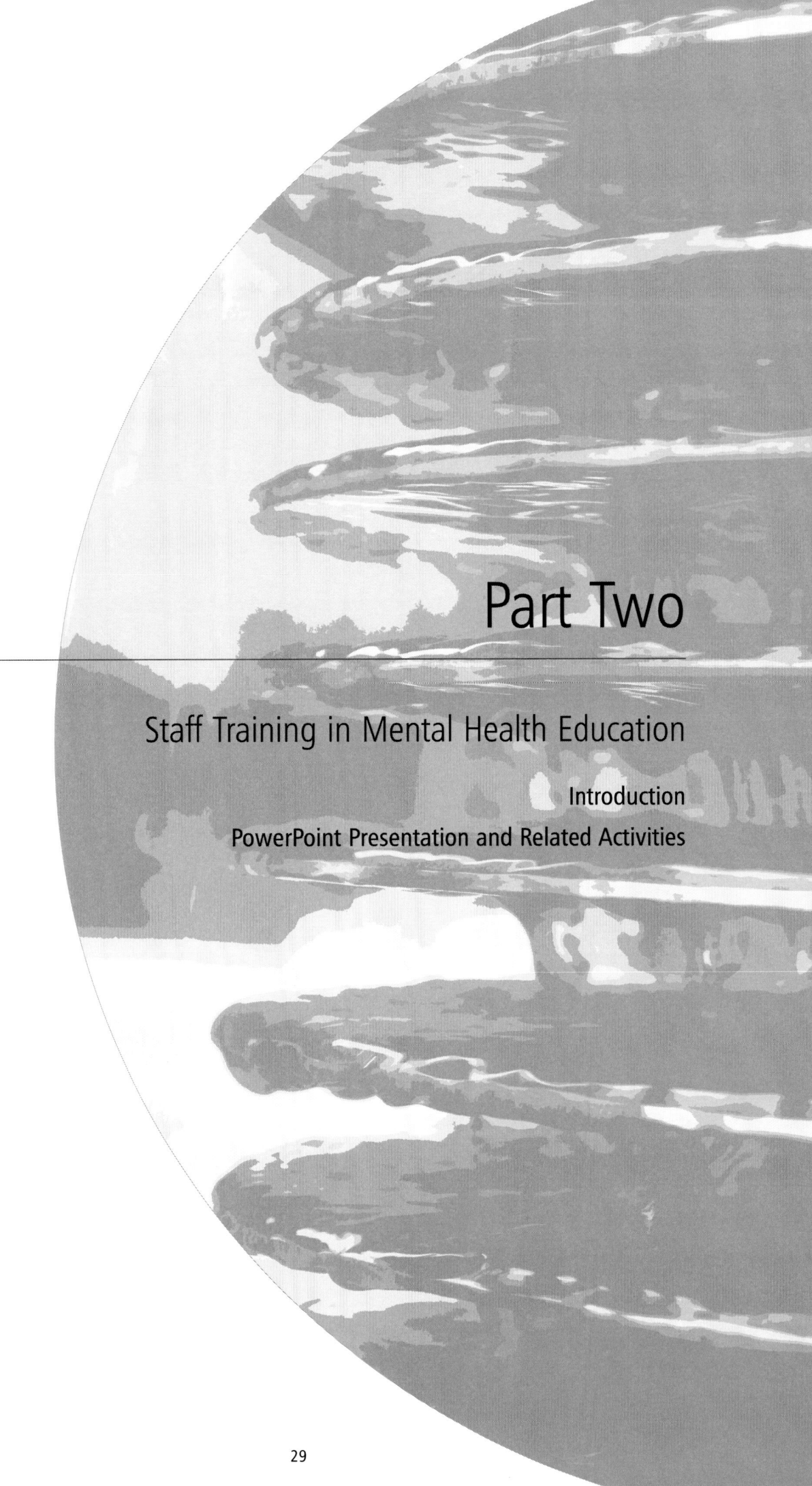

Part Two

Staff Training in Mental Health Education

Introduction

PowerPoint Presentation and Related Activities

Introduction

The PowerPoint presentation provides schools with an insight into preparing and delivering lessons on mental health. The slides provide an overview with facilitator notes and activities to promote greater understanding and knowledge of the topic areas.

Also included are activities intended for use with the pupils. The idea is that if staff experience some of the lessons they will be better prepared, as questions and issues will arise through discussion with colleagues.

The slides are intended to be used as INSET or twilight sessions, or a selection of them could be used to introduce the programme at a staff meeting.

The PowerPoint covers the following:

- What is Mental Health? Definitions and an activity to explore understanding and knowledge.
- National drivers including No Health without Mental Health, 2011.
- Social and Emotional Aspects of Learning.
- Why is Mental Health Education important?
- Facts and Figures.
- Risk and Resilience.
- Mental Health Topic Areas.
- What the Programme Covers.
- Aims and Objectives of the Programme.
- Understanding Brain Function.
- Mental Illness on a Continuum.
- Mental Health Disorders.
- Ground rules.
- Teaching about Mental Health.
- Question and answer session.
- Five Ways to Wellbeing.

The Mental Health Handbook
for Primary School:

Raising Awareness of
Mental Health

Sometimes My Brain Hurts
Programme

Slide 1

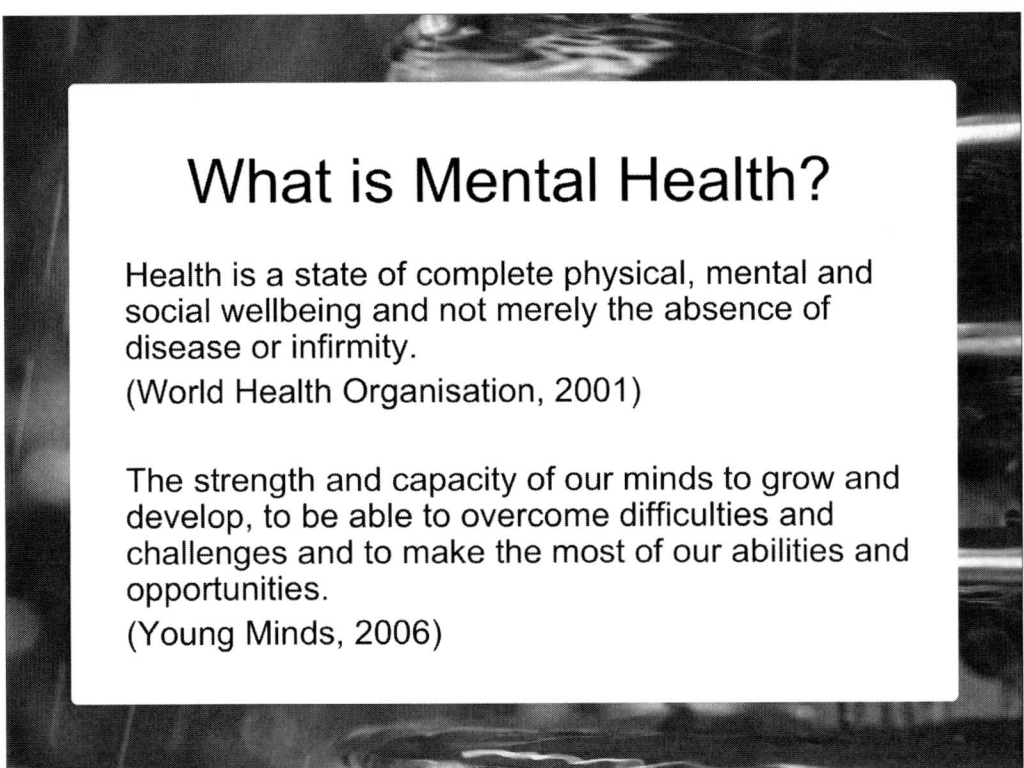

What is Mental Health?

Health is a state of complete physical, mental and social wellbeing and not merely the absence of disease or infirmity.
(World Health Organisation, 2001)

The strength and capacity of our minds to grow and develop, to be able to overcome difficulties and challenges and to make the most of our abilities and opportunities.
(Young Minds, 2006)

Facilitator Notes for Slide 2 and 3

These are just two definitions of mental health and it is interesting to note that the World Health Organisation has not revised its definition since 1948.

Activity Linked to Slides 2 and 3

Staff should be encouraged to explore their own understanding of mental health and what it means to them. This could also incorporate the use of language, both correct terms and derogatory language, as well as stigma and discrimination.

Following discussion in pairs take feedback.

Slide 3 is then introduced as it clarifies what is understood by mental illness. This will be explored further in later slides. Its main function here is to determine the difference between mental health and mental ill health.

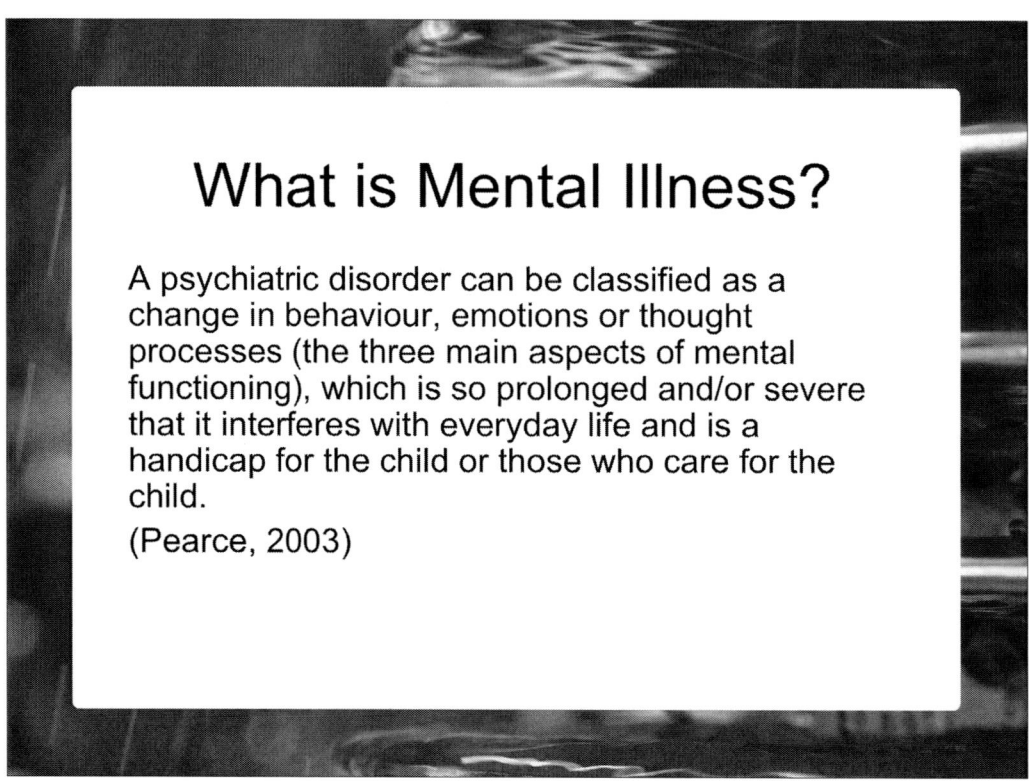

What is Mental Illness?

A psychiatric disorder can be classified as a change in behaviour, emotions or thought processes (the three main aspects of mental functioning), which is so prolonged and/or severe that it interferes with everyday life and is a handicap for the child or those who care for the child.

(Pearce, 2003)

Slide 3

National Initiatives

- No Health Without Mental Health, 2011.
- Targeted Mental Health in Schools, 2008-2011.
- Healthy Schools Plus, 2010.
- Revised Ofsted Framework, 2009.
- National Institute of Clinical Excellence, 2008.
- The Children's Plan: Building brighter futures, 2007.
- Every Child Matters, 2004.
- National Service Framework, 2003.
- Social and Emotional Aspects of Learning, 2003.

Facilitator Notes for Slide 4

There is no statutory requirement to teach about mental health in schools. The documents highlighted on the slide are many and varied and before the last election there was a cross party agreement regarding the teaching of personal, social and health education and a commitment to ensure that it became statutory. However, this commitment was never fulfilled.

The National Institute of Clinical Excellence (NICE) was asked by the Department of Health to provide guidance for schools and highlighted the importance of front line staff having adequate education, support and guidance to enable them to promote positive emotional and mental wellbeing for the pupils they work with.

Activity for Slide 4

Consider in groups how mental health could be introduced into the curriculum, where it fits and who should deliver it, what skills they will require, how much should be introduced, at what stage and for how long, and so on.

Ask what is currently provided and who leads on it. Take feedback.

No Health Without Mental Health

- More people will have good mental health by starting well, developing well, working well, living well and ageing well.
- More people with mental health problems will recover.
- More people with mental health problems will have good physical health.
- More people will have positive experiences of care and support.
- Fewer people will suffer avoidable harm.
- Fewer people will experience stigma and discrimination by increasing public understanding.
(Department of Health, 2011)

Facilitator Notes for Slide 5

This is a cross-government mental health strategy for people of all ages.

The slide highlights the six shared objectives which underpin the framework.

The mental health of children and young people is to be made a key part of the strategy with money being channelled into early intervention, including talking therapies for young people.

Activity Linked to Slide 5

The group could be asked for their thoughts on the proposed objectives and whether they might add additional ones.

Social and Emotional Aspects of Learning

- Self-awareness.
- Motivation.
- Managing feelings.
- Empathy.
- Social skills.

Facilitator Notes for Slide 6

Background information about SEAL:

- It is a whole-school approach although many schools have selected   certain topic areas to focus upon and there is a separate section that may   be used during anti-bullying week.

- Much of the material is based upon the 1995 book by Daniel Goleman   entitled Emotional Intelligence.

- It was introduced with government backing in 2003. Although it fits well into the PSHE agenda it is not a statutory requirement.

- The materials are extensive, including assemblies, Circle Time activities   and lesson plans. There are also activities for teaching staff, parents and   governors.

Activity Linked to Slide 6

Ask participants to review what works well and how SEAL activities or lessons could be extended to include material on mental health.

Ask participants to discuss how it is currently implemented, its effectiveness and approaches, staff attitudes and so on. For example, does it depend upon certain individuals?

Why is Mental Health Education Important?

- To raise awareness.
- Reduce stigma.
- Enable discussion using appropriate language.
- Promote access to support.
- Highlight the importance of early intervention.

Facilitator Notes for Slide 7

Many key mental health charities highlight the points on the slide as their priorities. These include:

- Young Minds.
- The Mental Health Foundation.
- Mental Health First Aid England.

Activity Linked to Slide 7

Participants should complete the mental health quiz that forms part of the lesson plan for Year 5 pupils. The quiz can be found at the end of this section. This will form the basis for the discussion and again re-examine some attitudes and understanding within the group.

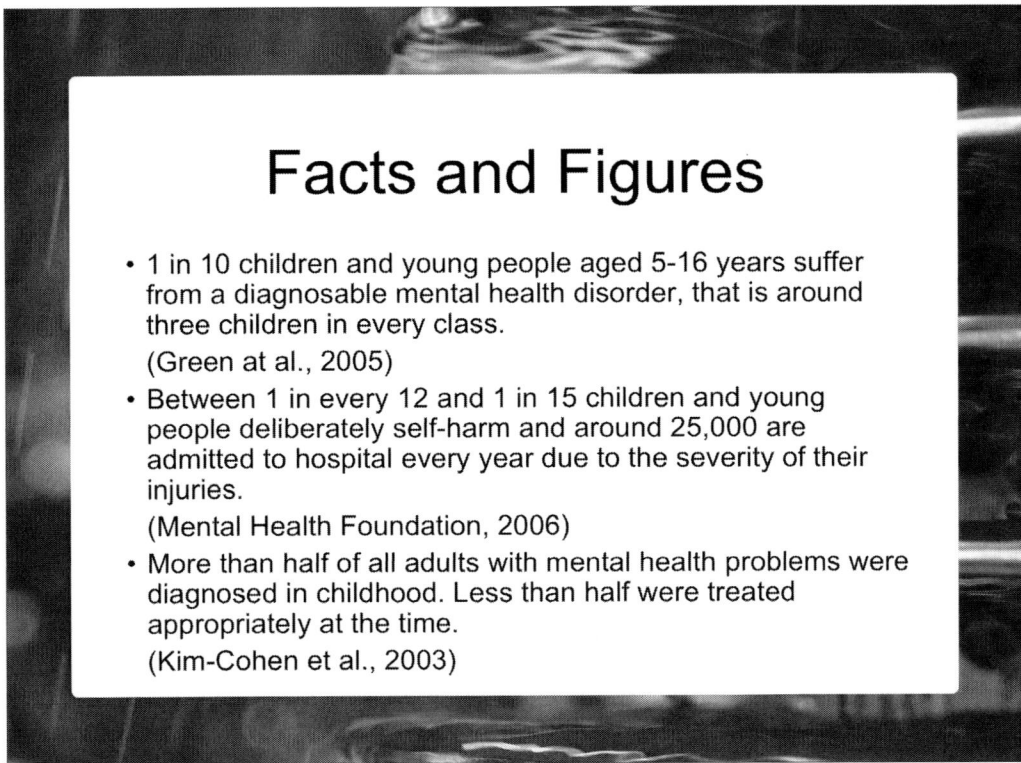

Facts and Figures

- 1 in 10 children and young people aged 5-16 years suffer from a diagnosable mental health disorder, that is around three children in every class.
(Green at al., 2005)
- Between 1 in every 12 and 1 in 15 children and young people deliberately self-harm and around 25,000 are admitted to hospital every year due to the severity of their injuries.
(Mental Health Foundation, 2006)
- More than half of all adults with mental health problems were diagnosed in childhood. Less than half were treated appropriately at the time.
(Kim-Cohen et al., 2003)

Facilitator Notes for Slides 8 and 9

This background information and the quiz answers from the previous slide are intended to increase awareness, knowledge and understanding in order for staff to lead the programme.

Facts and figures should be presented to illustrate the importance of talking about mental health in schools. Reference should be made to the Unicef report from 2007 when young people in the UK revealed how unhappy they were feeling.

There has been a significant increase in the amount of self-harm and depression in young people and perhaps more alarmingly among primary aged children.

Activity Linked to Slides 8 and 9

Staff are given the Facts and Figures handout, which is at the end of the session, and asked to reflect upon their reaction to the facts and figures. Does this fit with

Facts and Figures

- Nearly 80,000 children and young people suffer from severe depression. Over 8,000 children aged under ten years old suffer from severe depression.
  (Office for National Statistics, 2004)
- 45% of children in care have a mental health disorder. These are some of the most vulnerable people in our society.
  (Meltzer et al., 2003)
- 95% of imprisoned young offenders have a mental health disorder. Many of them are struggling with more than one disorder.
  (Office for National Statistics, 1997)

Slide 9

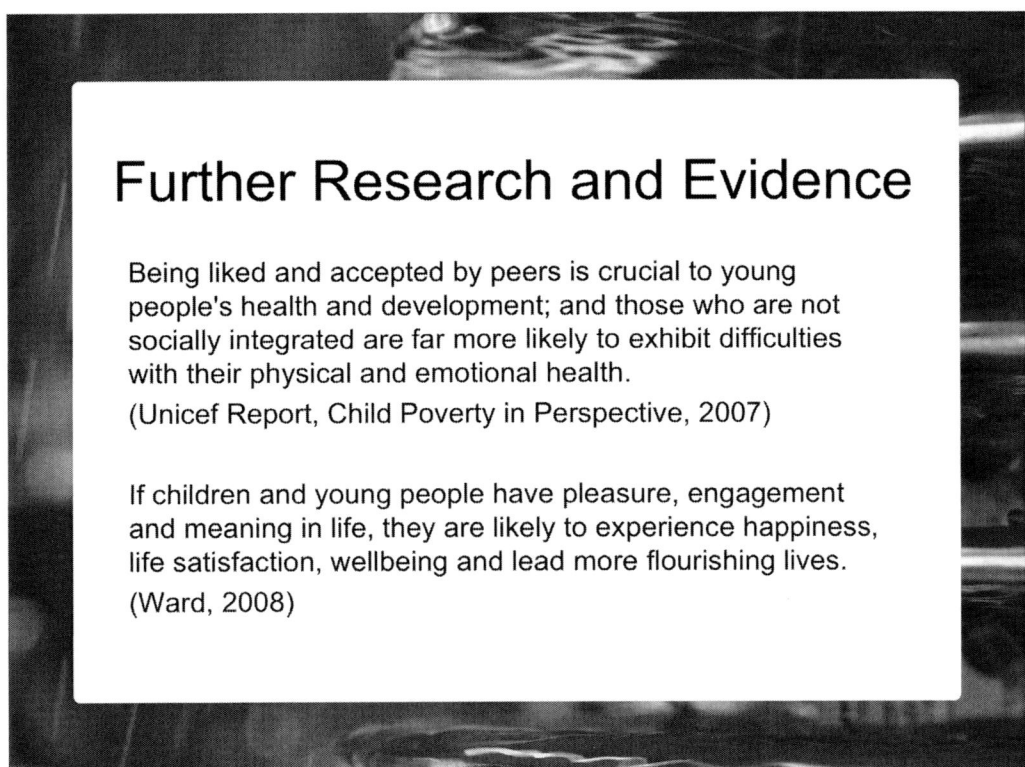

Further Research and Evidence

Being liked and accepted by peers is crucial to young people's health and development; and those who are not socially integrated are far more likely to exhibit difficulties with their physical and emotional health.
(Unicef Report, Child Poverty in Perspective, 2007)

If children and young people have pleasure, engagement and meaning in life, they are likely to experience happiness, life satisfaction, wellbeing and lead more flourishing lives.
(Ward, 2008)

Facilitator Notes for Slide 10

Reference was made to the Unicef document in the notes for slides 8 and 9. The research highlighted how the UK compares with other countries regarding children and young people's levels of contentment, happiness and optimism about their futures. The evidence suggested that children and young people living and growing up in the UK are not as satisfied with their lives as their European counterparts, and as Ward points out, unless they have some meaning and happiness, they will not flourish. These facts contribute to the argument that we should be taking better care of children and young people's mental and emotional wellbeing and ensuring that they have opportunities to talk about how they are feeling.

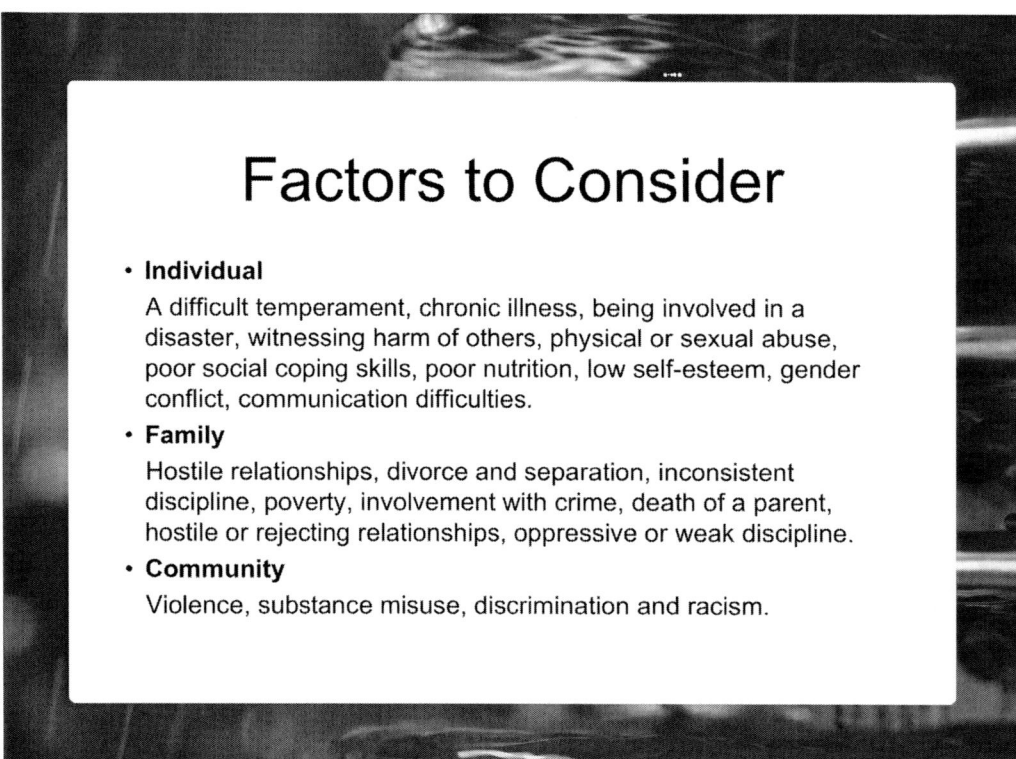

Facilitator Notes for Slides 11 and 12

There are many factors that contribute to a young person's mental and emotional wellbeing. They may be divided into three main categories:

1. Individual.

2. Family.

3. Community.

Activity Linked to Slides 11 and 12

Participants are asked to consider what influences young people's emotional health and wellbeing. They are then provided with a list of factors on the Risk and Resilience handout and encouraged to identify a few of their own.

When the activity is completed show Slide 12, which provides an example of categorisation.

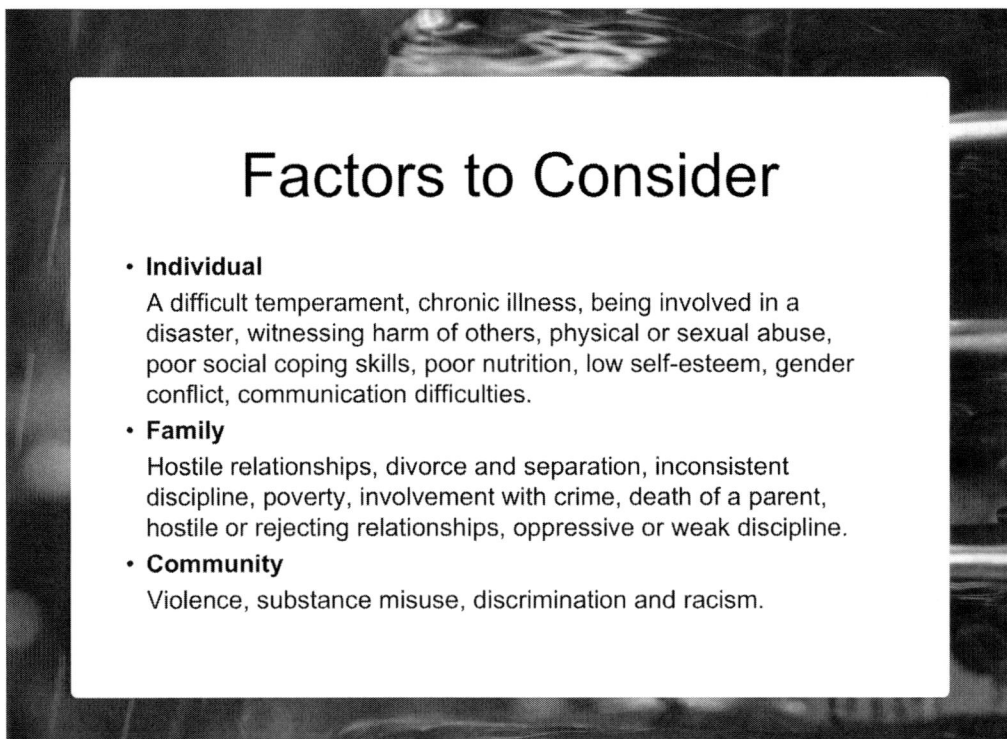

Factors to Consider

- **Individual**

  A difficult temperament, chronic illness, being involved in a disaster, witnessing harm of others, physical or sexual abuse, poor social coping skills, poor nutrition, low self-esteem, gender conflict, communication difficulties.

- **Family**

  Hostile relationships, divorce and separation, inconsistent discipline, poverty, involvement with crime, death of a parent, hostile or rejecting relationships, oppressive or weak discipline.

- **Community**

  Violence, substance misuse, discrimination and racism.

Slide 12

Diamond Nine Exercise

Pupils:
- understand the difference between mental health and mental illness
- learn correct terms to describe mental illness
- are aware that mental ill health can affect anyone
- can ask questions in a safe environment
- are aware that depression is not a choice
- can dispel any myths associated with mental health
- understand that recovery from mental illness is not only possible but most likely
- are aware that there is always someone to talk to
- learn what can promote positive mental health.

Activity Linked to Slide 13

Working in small groups, participants are asked to arrange the statements in the diamonds in order of importance, using the page at the end of this section.

This activity is one that will be used with the pupils and helps to establish what their understanding of mental health is.

During the activity it will be useful to consider what the pupils responses might be to the statements.

Key messages from research highlight the importance of recovery, and also that early intervention is important.

Statements should be discussed in relation to each other and consideration given as to whether it is more important to raise awareness, focus upon improving access to help, or on promoting the correct terminology to reduce stigma.

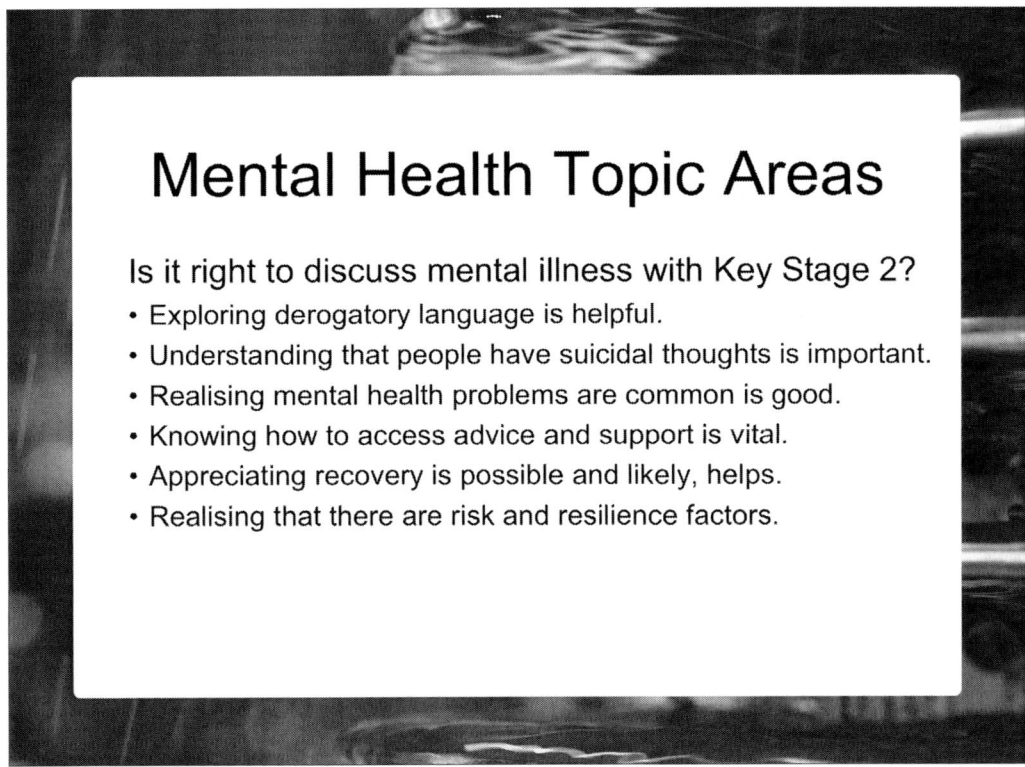

Mental Health Topic Areas

Is it right to discuss mental illness with Key Stage 2?
- Exploring derogatory language is helpful.
- Understanding that people have suicidal thoughts is important.
- Realising mental health problems are common is good.
- Knowing how to access advice and support is vital.
- Appreciating recovery is possible and likely, helps.
- Realising that there are risk and resilience factors.

Facilitator Notes for Slide 14

There is evidence from research to suggest that it is helpful to discuss mental health problems with young people (MHFA, 2010).

Activity Linked to Slide 14

The statements should be read out from the slide and participants asked for their views, either agreeing or disagreeing. The discussion is aimed at promoting knowledge and confidence as well as dispelling any misunderstandings.

What the Programme Covers

- What is mental health?
- Why it is important.
- What goes wrong?
- What helps and what does not?
- How to access help.
- How it is portrayed.
- How to promote positive mental health.

Activity Linked to Slide 15

Staff can discuss what they would feel happy teaching from the above list on the slide. It is interesting to compare individual opinions. The aim is to reach a consensus and develop a way, with agreement and commitment, to take the work forward and enable the programme to be successful.

Explore with staff how much they know about the support for mental health and wellbeing that is available in their area.

Discuss and plan how they will provide support for each other while delivering the programme.

Aims and Objectives of the Programme

- Create a better understanding of mental health.
- Raise awareness of mental health issues.
- Explore what promotes positive mental health.
- Examine what impacts in a negative way.
- Understand how early identification and intervention helps.
- Provide opportunities for discussion.
- Protect children from inappropriate media portrayal of mental health problems.
- Reduce stigma.

Activities Linked to Slides 16 and 17

Talk through the points on the slide and encourage discussion.

Acknowledge that while there are common themes, each establishment will have its own issues. Some schools place a higher emphasis on pastoral support and enable more open discussion of sensitive subjects.

When you consider how many people have mental health problems at some stage in their lives, some of the children in each class will be affected as well as their parents and teaching staff!

Discuss if any of these aims and objectives are not necessary for your establishment.

Are there any aims and objectives that should be added?

The facilitator should then show Slide 17 which illustrates how important it is that staff working with children and young people have a good understanding of mental health.

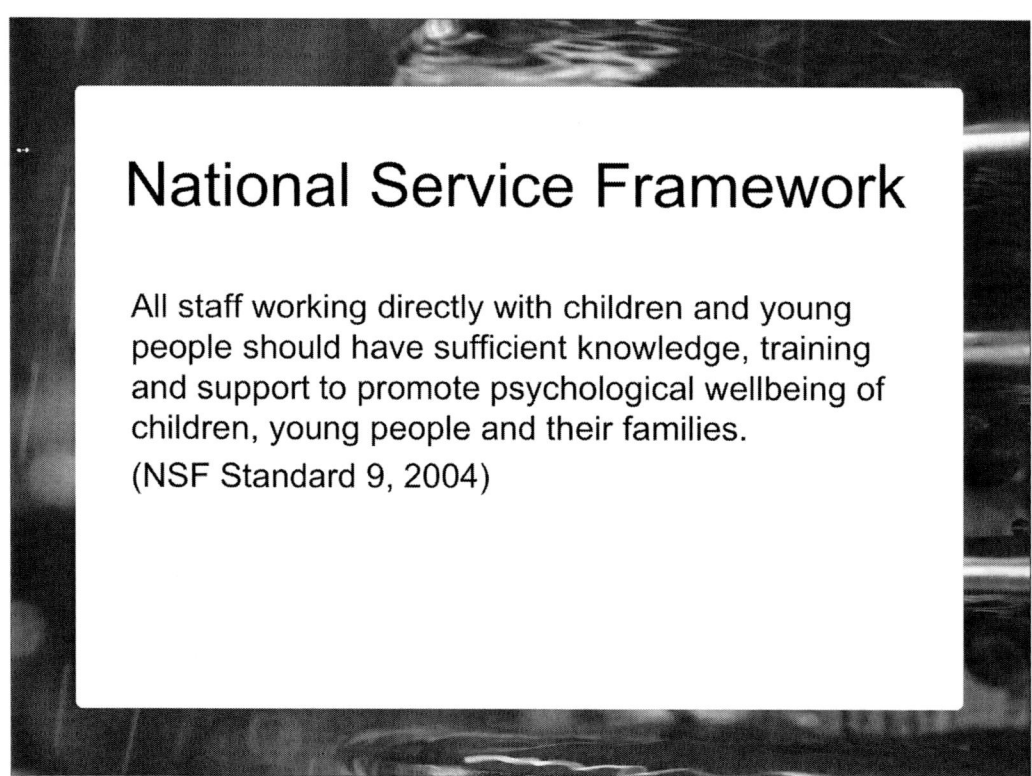

National Service Framework

All staff working directly with children and young people should have sufficient knowledge, training and support to promote psychological wellbeing of children, young people and their families.

(NSF Standard 9, 2004)

Slide 17

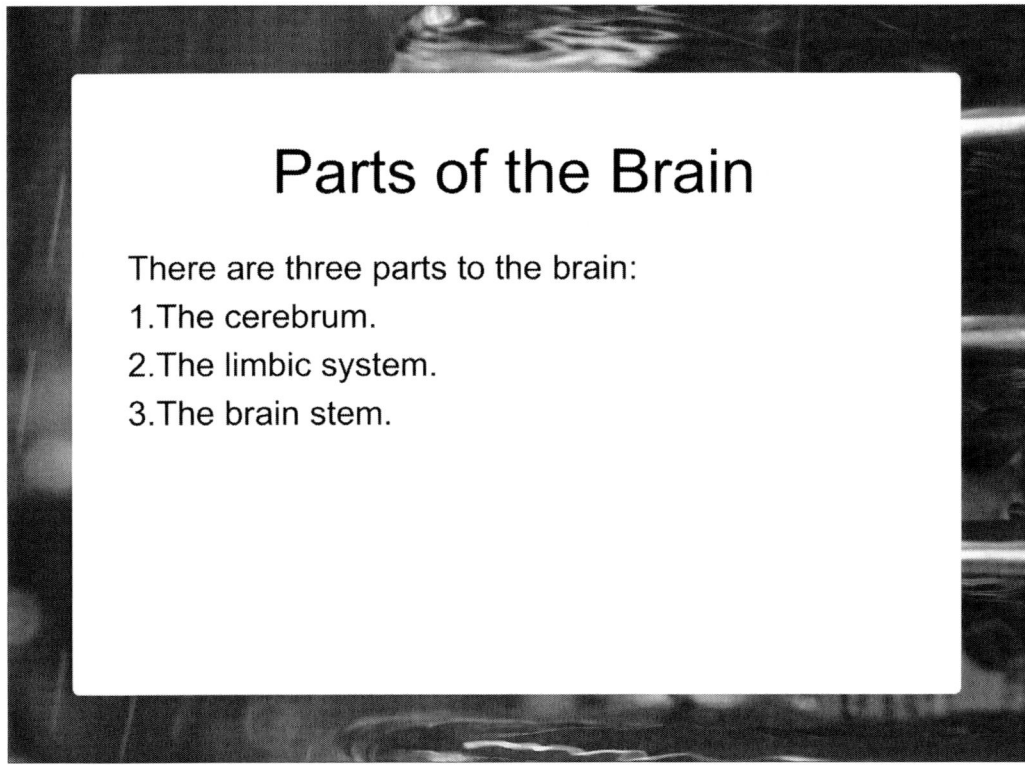

Parts of the Brain

There are three parts to the brain:
1. The cerebrum.
2. The limbic system.
3. The brain stem.

Facilitator Notes for Slide 18

The cerebrum: The cerebrum or cortex is the largest part of the human brain, associated with higher brain function such as thought and action. The cerebral cortex is divided into four sections : the frontal lobe, parietal lobe, occipital lobe and temporal lobe.

Limbic system: The limbic system, often referred to as the 'emotional brain', is found buried within the cerebrum. In evolutionary terms the structure is rather old. This system contains the thalamus, hypothalamus, amygdala and hippocampus.

Brain stem: Underneath the limbic system is the brain stem. This structure is responsible for basic vital life functions such as breathing, heartbeat, and blood pressure. Scientists say that this is the 'simplest' part of the human brain because the entire brain of animals such as reptiles (who appear early on the evolutionary scale) resemble our brain stem.

It is helpful to have some understanding of brain function especially when considering what happens when people experience anxiety. From a teachers point of view if a child or young person in their class is experiencing anxiety, then the limbic or most basic part of their brain which focuses solely upon survival is functioning, whereas the higher cortex or cerebrum that deals with thoughts and reasoning is not.

During development a foetus forms synapses, and there is a rewiring and formation of new synapses during adolescence. This is a time when attachments are formed, and many emerging mental health problems might start to manifest at this stage, but will be difficult to identify because early signs of psychosis look very similar to normal adolescent moodiness and challenging behaviour, with altered eating and sleeping patterns and withdrawal from things that they used to enjoy.

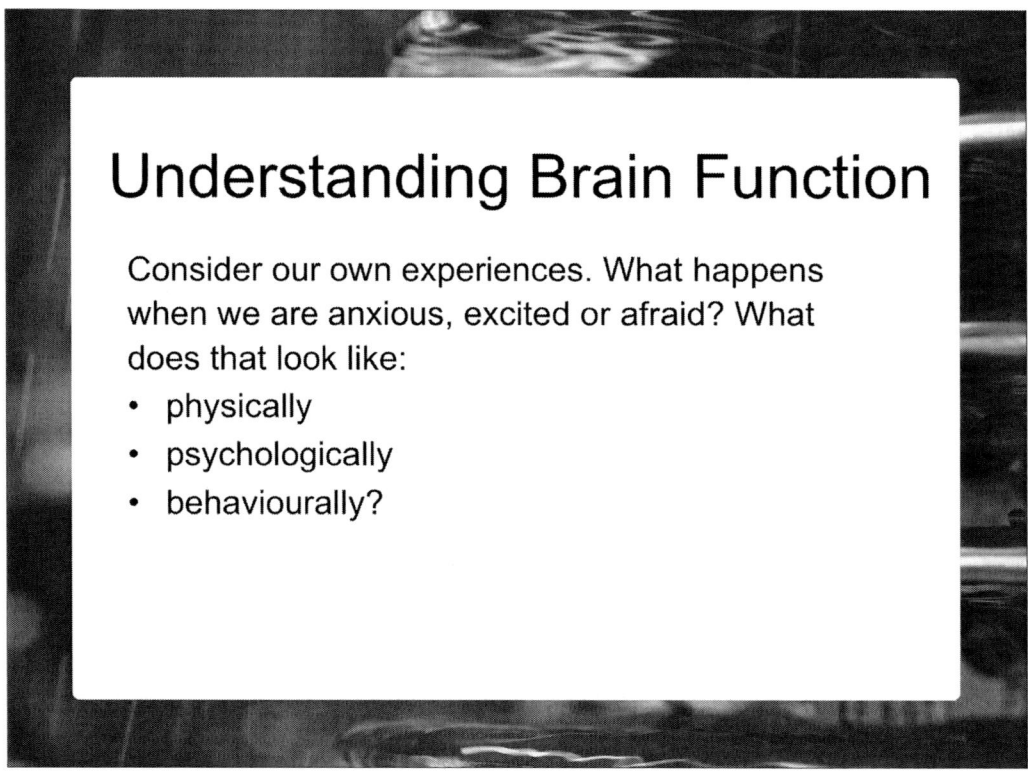

Understanding Brain Function

Consider our own experiences. What happens when we are anxious, excited or afraid? What does that look like:

- physically
- psychologically
- behaviourally?

Facilitator Notes for Slide 19

Explain what happens when we are anxious, highlighting that anxiety is normal.

Basically, anxiety can vary from mild unease to a full panic attack when an individual would not be able to think rationally.

Anxiety is on the increase among young people as they worry about getting good grades in school.

The effects of anxiety can be divided into three categories:

1. Physical – rapid heartbeat, shortness of breath, dizziness, sweating, dry mouth, nausea, aches and pains, shaking.

2. Psychological - unrealistic or excessive fear and worry about past or future events, mind racing or going blank, loss of memory, difficulty making decisions, confusion, impatience, anger, restlessness, sleep disturbance, vivid dreams, unwanted unpleasant thoughts.

3. Behavioural - avoiding situations, repetitive, compulsive checking of lights, washing   hands many times and so on, urges to escape difficult situations.

Activity Linked to Slide 19

Discuss a time when members of the group felt anxious. Points to consider:

- How did they feel?
- What were their thoughts?
- How did they behave or react?

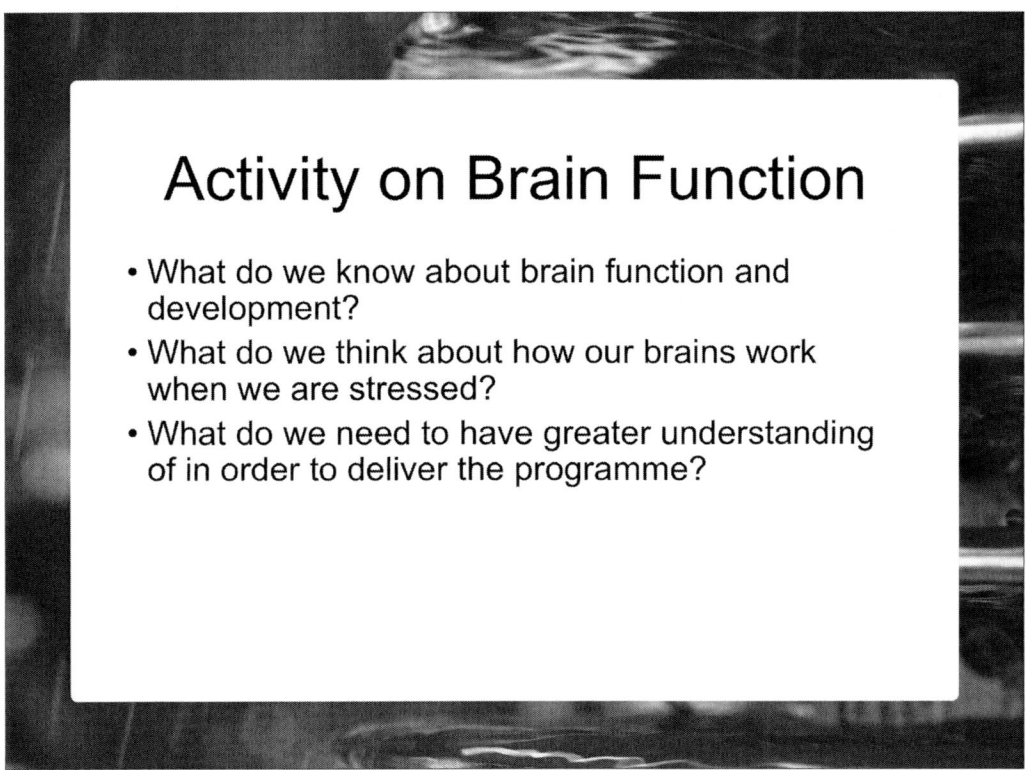

Activity on Brain Function

- What do we know about brain function and development?
- What do we think about how our brains work when we are stressed?
- What do we need to have greater understanding of in order to deliver the programme?

Activity Linked to Slide 20

The facilitator provides the group with flipchart paper and poses these three questions for discussion.

The idea is that if we have a greater understanding of how our brains function it will provide greater insight into mental and emotional difficulties.

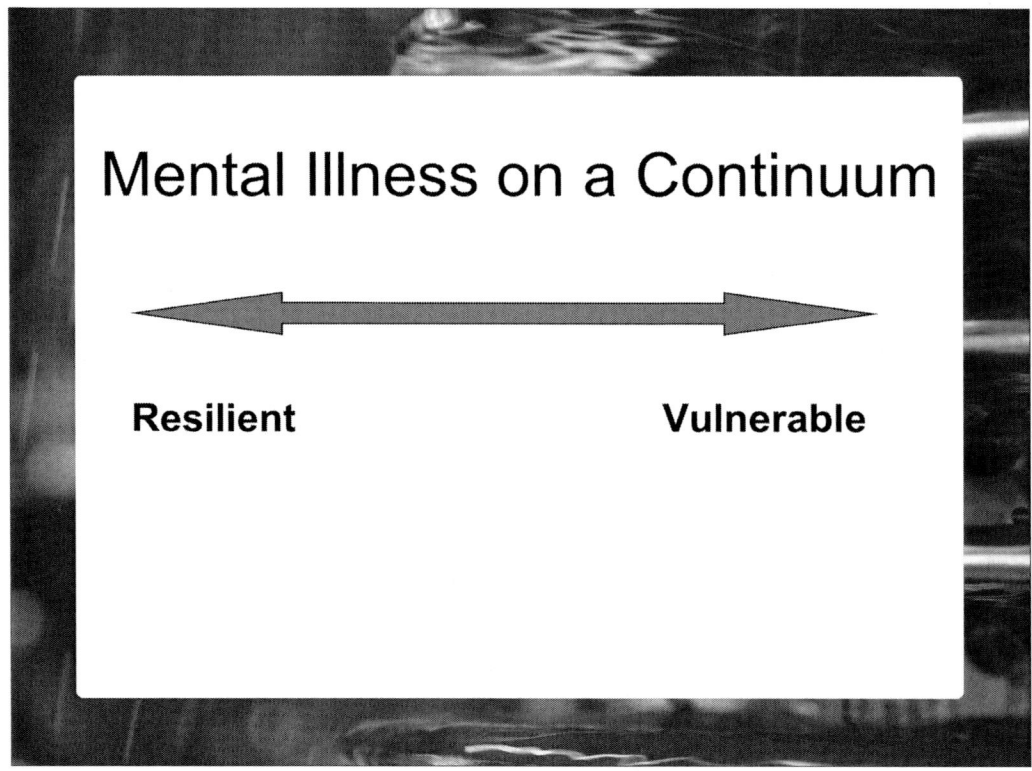

Facilitator Notes for Slide 21

Introduce the idea of mental health upon a continuum and facilitate a discussion around recovery and the fact that it is possible to have good mental and emotional wellbeing despite having a diagnosis of a mental health disorder.

The emphasis is on the fact that we all have mental health challenges and various things affect our equilibrium. At any time in our lives we may be moving along the continuum.

Activity Linked to Slide 21

Participants are asked to consider events and occurrences that would move them along the continuum.

The facilitator should make some suggestions such as bereavement pushing a person along towards the vulnerable end and winning the lottery placing you at the resilient end, or not?

Additional factors should be introduced and considered such as being made redundant, being bullied, achieving success in exams, feeling safe and secure and having someone to talk to who you can trust.

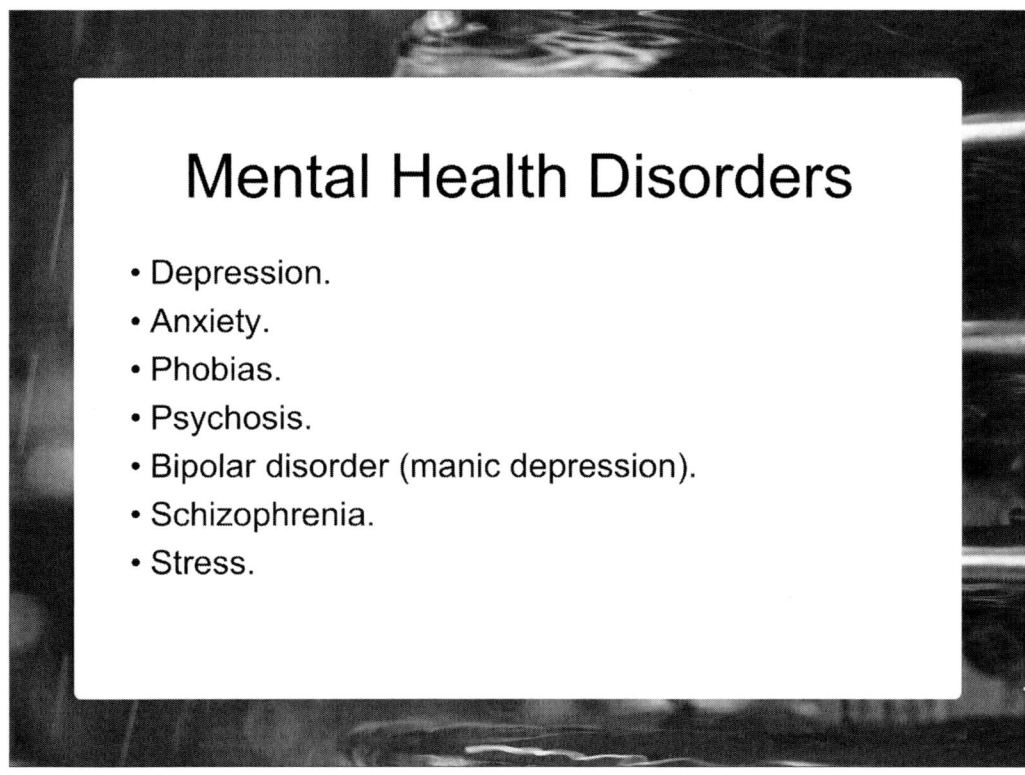

Mental Health Disorders

- Depression.
- Anxiety.
- Phobias.
- Psychosis.
- Bipolar disorder (manic depression).
- Schizophrenia.
- Stress.

Facilitator Notes for Slide 22 and 23

Distribute copies of the Glossary of Terms from Part Four before showing both the slides.

It is worth pointing out to participants that the programme is not about teaching teachers to become therapists but rather to increase their knowledge and understanding of mental health and mental ill health.

A key message here is that many mental health problems coexist and it is not about being able to diagnose people but rather to identify and help with the signs and symptoms they might be experiencing.

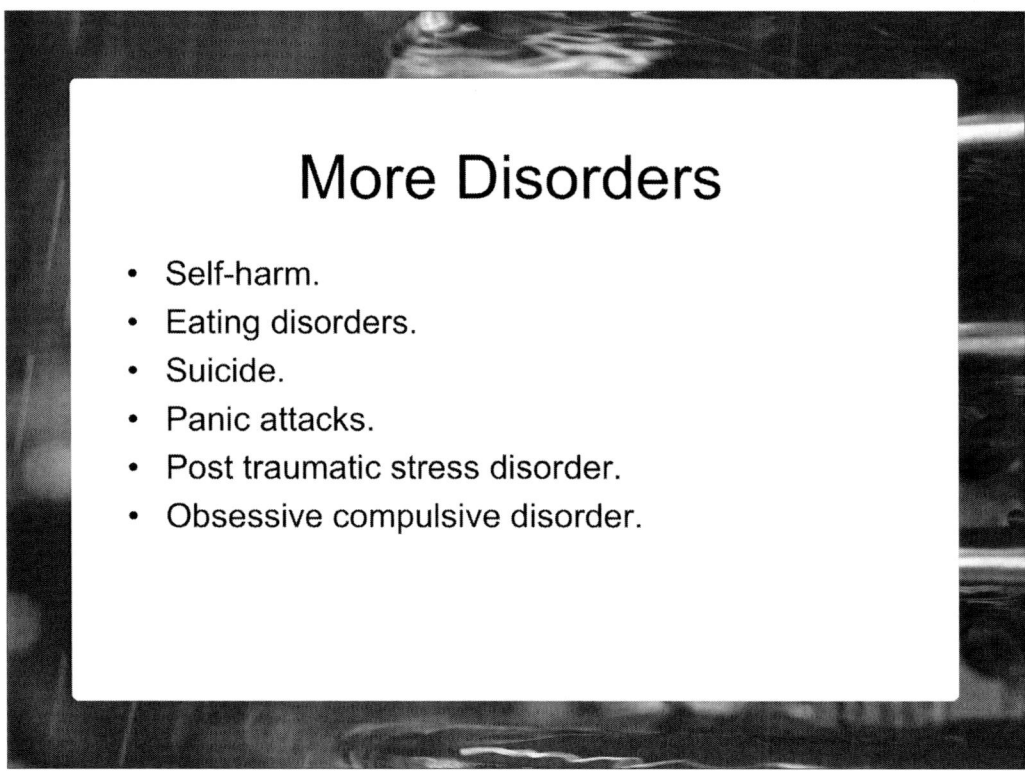

Activities Linked to Slides 22 and 23

A list of symptoms cards (Signs and Symptoms of Mental Illness found at the back of this section) should be distributed to the group who are then asked to determine which disorder they relate to. The idea is to introduce the fact that mental health is very complex and more often than not there is co-morbidity with many individuals experiencing, for example, depression along with anxiety and therefore both sets of symptoms. The list of symptoms cards is not exhaustive and participants could be asked to contribute additional ones.

The pupils are asked to organize these cards into four categories.

- Anxiety
- Depression
- Self Harm
- Psychosis

What will emerge is that many symptoms overlap different disorders.

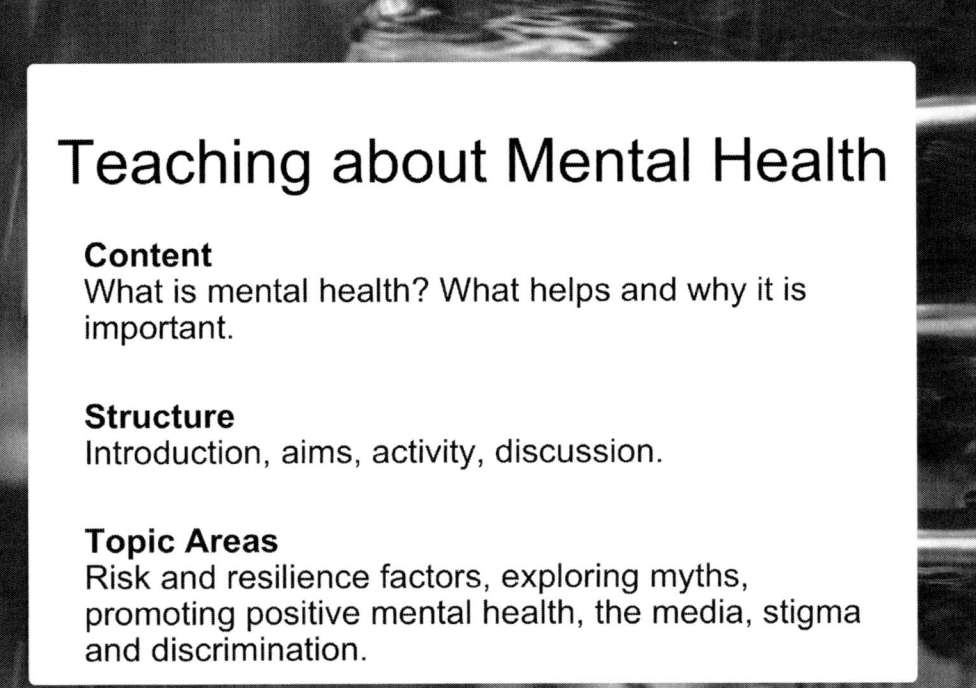

Teaching about Mental Health

Content
What is mental health? What helps and why it is important.

Structure
Introduction, aims, activity, discussion.

Topic Areas
Risk and resilience factors, exploring myths, promoting positive mental health, the media, stigma and discrimination.

Facilitator Notes for Slide 24

Introduce the slide and emphasise the various aspects of the programme. Staff are then encouraged to discuss what they would feel happy and confident teaching and what they might feel uncomfortable with. There are no right or wrong answers.

Activity Linked to Slide 24

Staff are given the lesson plans as suggested below and encouraged to become familiar with the material. They should work in year groups so that each person gains a better understanding of the material for their particular class and can consider some of the issues that might arise.

They should work in pairs and take it in turns to present the lesson to colleagues, if time permits. This will also inform the question and answer section and the concerns of some staff that they will be asked questions that they cannot answer.

An example for each group would be:

- Year 3. Finding Support (Theme Two: Lesson 2)
- Year 4. Language for Mental Health (Theme Two: Lesson 2)
- Year 5. What helps and What Does Not? (Theme Two: Lesson 1)
- Year 6. The Cost of Mental Health (Theme Three: Lesson 1).

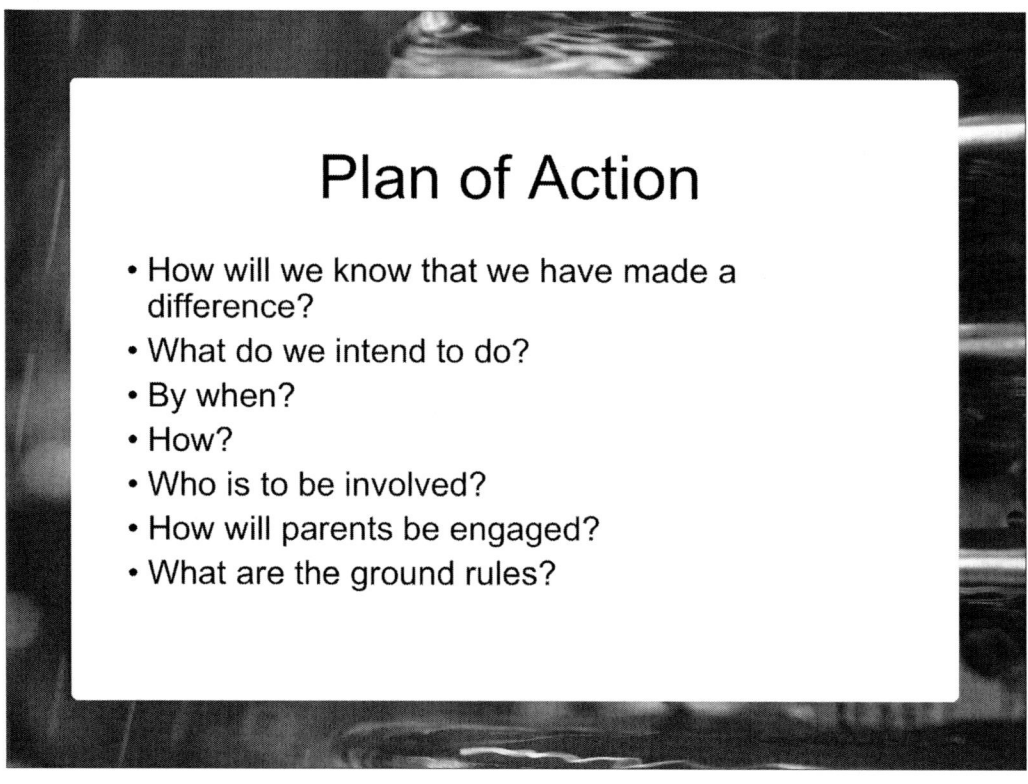

Plan of Action

- How will we know that we have made a difference?
- What do we intend to do?
- By when?
- How?
- Who is to be involved?
- How will parents be engaged?
- What are the ground rules?

Facilitator Notes for Slide 25

Pose the questions on the slide to the group for discussion.

A consideration might be for parents to be invited into school one evening to view the proposed resources and ask questions and voice their concerns.

Participants to discuss what they will do, who will do it and when, how they can measure the impact of the work and how they will know they have made a difference.

Staff could be asked to develop ideas around how they will measure outcomes of the programme.

A pupil evaluation form, which can be found at the end of the section, should be issued for discussion.

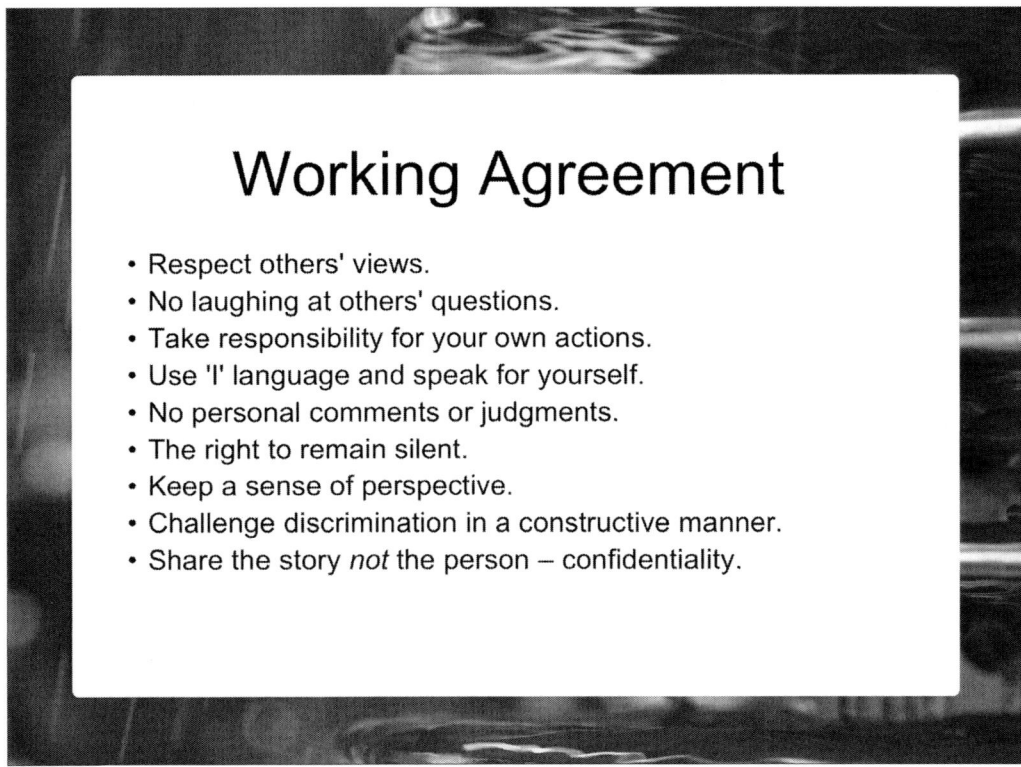

Working Agreement

- Respect others' views.
- No laughing at others' questions.
- Take responsibility for your own actions.
- Use 'I' language and speak for yourself.
- No personal comments or judgments.
- The right to remain silent.
- Keep a sense of perspective.
- Challenge discrimination in a constructive manner.
- Share the story *not* the person – confidentiality.

Activity Linked to Slide 26

Discuss the slide with suggestions of ground rules and group agreements and ask staff for any additions or deletions.

If time allows draw on participants' experience and how they have developed classroom rules and agreements with pupils. Explore what works best.

Also highlight that the subject of mental health is sensitive so the agreement is particularly important to ensure that everyone feels safe.

Answering Questions

Positive

- Pupils will feel confident and able to ask further questions.
- Pupils receive age appropriate answers in language they understand.

Negative

- Member of staff is not sure or feels embarrassed and gives wrong answer.
- Member of staff presents judgmental attitude.
- Pupils feel more confused and anxious.

Facilitator Notes for Slide 27

Discuss participants' feelings about answering pupils' questions. Are there any specific worries?

It is worth highlighting that many health professional in the world of mental health have disagreements over diagnosis and therefore staff do not have to have all the answers. They could suggest a follow-up activity for the children to research some of the answers on the internet and find them together.

Activity Linked to Slide 27

Staff to complete the Reality or Myth activity for Year 5, Theme One, Lesson 2 and the Our Needs cards activity for Year 6, Theme Two, Lesson 1.

Answering Questions

- Can children have mental health problems?
- Why do people suffer from depression?
- Is recovery possible if you have a mental health problem?
- Are mental health problems common?
- Why do people self-harm?
- What is schizophrenia?
- Are people with mental health problems dangerous?
- If my parents are mentally unwell will I become ill too?

Activity Linked to Slide 28

Staff are asked to consider the questions on the slide as well as thinking of as many questions as they can and practise asking and answering in pairs to gain confidence.

Discuss further what participants found the most difficult, highlighting how important it is to practise answering questions to become familiar with the language and gain confidence.

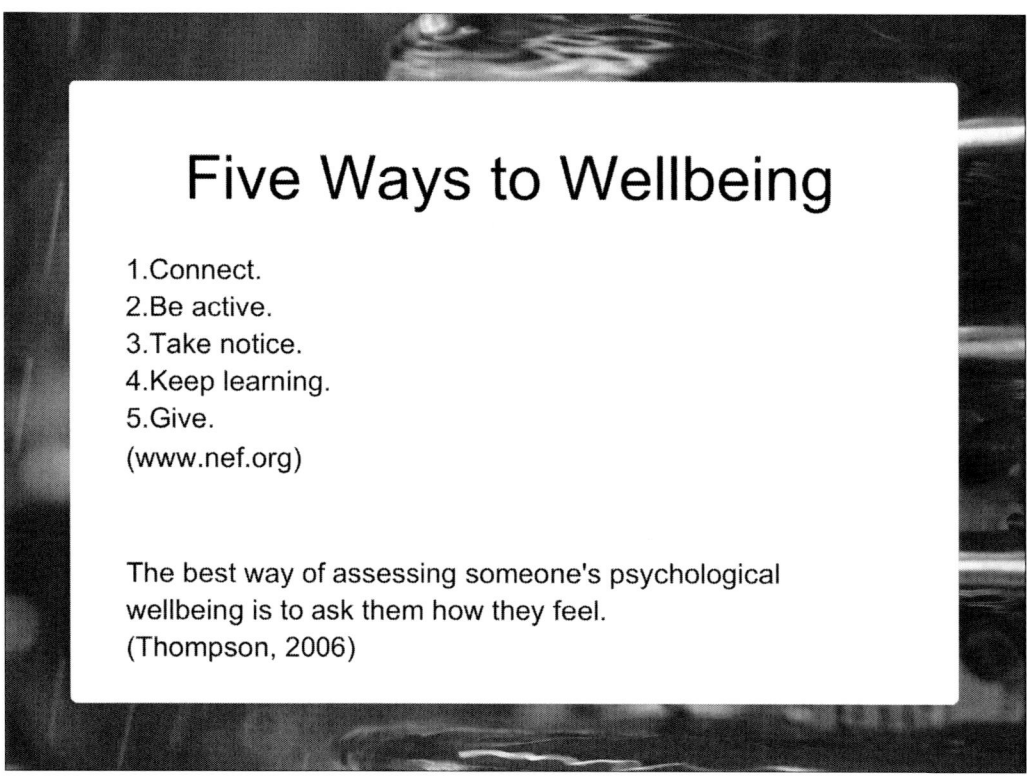

Five Ways to Wellbeing

1. Connect.
2. Be active.
3. Take notice.
4. Keep learning.
5. Give.
(www.nef.org)

The best way of assessing someone's psychological wellbeing is to ask them how they feel.
(Thompson, 2006)

Facilitator Notes for Slide 29

As groups may find it difficult talking about mental health problems it is a nice idea to end on a positive note.

Introduce the New Economics Foundation Five Ways to Wellbeing found on a handout at the end of this section.

Activity Linked to Slide 29

Ask the group to discuss how they connect, give, are active, keep learning, take notice and share with each other. A handout can be found at the end of this section.

Mental Health Quiz

Name:

Complete the following quiz.

Questions	True	False
1. 1 in 4 young people will experience a mental health problem at some stage in their lives.		
2. Mental health problems affect lazy people.		
3. Once you have a mental health problem you never recover.		
4. Girls have more eating disorders than boys.		
5. Depression lasts for years.		
6. Medication doesn't work.		
7. People stop self-harming when they get older.		
8. Everyone knows when a person is mentally unwell.		
9. Many more people have mental health problems than diabetes.		
10. Exercise and activity will improve mental health.		

TTI Mental Health Handbook

Mental Health Quiz Answers

Questions	Answers
1. 1 in 4 young people will experience a mental health problem at some stage in their lives.	True. Mental health problems are much more common than people realise and also many conditions go undiagnosed, so this figure is probably an underestimate.
2. Mental health problems affect lazy people.	False. There is widespread misunderstanding that mental health problems are in some way a choice and that if people are lazy they use depression as an excuse.
3. Once you have a mental health problem you never recover.	False. The vast majority of people with mental health problems will recover, there are some who may become unwell again and some who also have ongoing problems.
4. Girls have more eating disorders than boys.	True, although this might be because girls are more willing to admit to having a problem.
5. Depression lasts for years.	True and False. The condition is very variable and will alter for each individual so while some people may have a problem for a long time, others will recover very quickly.
6. Medication doesn't work.	True and False. Mental health problems are much more complex than physical ones and while specific medication works for some individuals it does not necessarily work for all and adjustment and trial of certain medication might have to be explored. Not everyone with a mental health problem will need medication as there are alternative therapies, such as counselling.
7. People stop self-harming when they get older.	False. Self-harming behaviour does not just affect young people there are much older people who continue to use it as a coping strategy.

Mental Health Quiz Answers (Cont)

Questions	Answers
8. Everyone knows when a person is mentally unwell.	False. Many people who have a mental health problem become very good at hiding it and if other people do not know how to recognise mental distress they completely miss the signs.
9. Many more people have mental health problems than diabetes.	True. Because diabetes does not carry the stigma associated with mental health problems it gets talked about, therefore most people believe it is more common than psychosis for example.
10. Exercise and activity will improve mental health.	True. There is much evidence to suggest that exercise promotes positive mental health in the way it improves physical health. Some GP surgeries actually prescribe exercise for people with mental health problems. When we exercise, the body produces endorphins that help to lift mood so it naturally follows that mental health will be improved.

Facts and Figures Handout

1 in 10 children and young people aged 5-16 years suffer from a diagnosable mental health disorder, that is, around three children in every class. ①

Between 1 in every 12 to 15 children and young people deliberately self-harm ② and around 25,000 are admitted to hospital every year due to the severity of their injuries. ③

More than half of all adults with mental health problems were diagnosed in childhood. Less than half were treated appropriately at the time. ④

Nearly 80,000 children and young people suffer from severe depression. ⑤

Over 8,000 children aged under 10 years old suffer from severe depression. ⑥

45% of children in care have a mental health disorder. These are some of the most vulnerable people in our society. ⑦

95% of imprisoned young offenders have a mental health disorder. Many of them are struggling with more than one disorder. ⑧

Sources

1. Green, H., McGinnity, A., Meltzer, H., et al. (2005) *Mental Health of Children and Young People in Great Britain.* London: Office for National Statistics.

2. Mental Health Foundation (2006) *Truth Hurts: Report of the National Inquiry into Self-Harm among Young People.* London: Mental Health Foundation.

3. Fox, C. & Hawton, K. (2004) *Deliberate Self-Harm in Adolescence.* London: Jessica Kingsley Publishers.

4. Kim-Cohen, J., Caspi, A., Moffitt, T. E. et al. (2003) '*Prior Juvenile Diagnosis in Adults with Mental Disorder*'. Archives of General Psychiatry, Vol. 60, p.709-717.

5. & 6. Office for National Statistics (2004) *Census 2001: National Report for England and Wales.* London: Office for National Statistics.

7. Meltzer, H., Gatward, R., Corbin, T. et al. (2003) *The Mental Health of Young People Looked After by Local Authorities in England.* London: Stationery Office.

8. Office for National Statistics (1997) *Psychiatric Morbidity Among Young Offenders in England and Wales.* London: Office for National Statistics.

Risk and Resilience

Place the risk factors under the appropriate category adding any other factors that you can think of.

Individual	Family	Community

Violence.

Divorce and separation.

Being involved in a disaster.

Hostile relationships.

Witnessing harm of others.

Substance misuse.

Poverty.

Low self-esteem.

Physical or sexual abuse.

A difficult temperament.

Chronic illness.

Discrimination and racism.

Poor social coping skills.

Poor nutrition.

Death of a parent.

Hostile or rejecting relationships.

Gender conflict.

Inconsistent discipline.

Involvement with crime.

Communication difficulties.

Oppressive or weak discipline.

Diamond Nine

I understand the difference between mental health and mental illness.

I have learned the correct terms to describe mental illness.

I am aware that mental ill health can affect anyone.

I can ask questions in a safe environment.

I am aware that depression is not a choice.

I can dispel any myths associated with mental health.

I understand that recovery from mental illness is not only possible but most likely.

I am aware that there is always someone to talk to.

I have learned what can promote positive mental health.

Signs and Symptoms of Mental Illness

Loss of appetite.	Feeling very worried.
Overeating.	Sweating.
Difficulty sleeping.	Heart racing.
Sleeping too much.	Getting angry very quickly.
Crying.	Avoiding situations.
Very low mood.	Panicking.
Not enjoying anything.	Feeling sick.
Hearing voices.	Hurting yourself.
Seeing things that are not there.	Cutting yourself.
Thinking everyone is against you.	Not eating.
Losing touch with reality.	Making yourself sick.
Feeling that things are slowed down or speeded up.	Exercising excessively.
Staying in all the time.	Putting yourself down all the time.
Loss of memory.	

Anxiety	Depression
Self-harm	Psychosis

Pupil Evaluation Form

I.	Did the lessons in the programme help you to understand a little bit more about mental health? Yes No
2.	Which session did you prefer most? Please explain why.
3.	Please tick all the subjects you have learned about: • Comparing mental health and physical health. • Identifying mental and physical ill health. • Healthy minds and healthy brains. • Finding support. • What happens when you become unwell? • Language for mental health.
4.	Is there anything else you would like to learn but did not cover in this programme?

Five Ways to Wellbeing

1. Connect

Connecting with family, friends and people around you at home, school, and in your community will enrich and support you every day.

2. Be Active

Exercising makes you feel good. Find something you enjoy such as dancing or going for a walk.

3. Take Notice

Be curious and ask questions, remark on the unusual, savour the moment, be aware of the world around you. Reflecting on your experiences will help you to appreciate what matters to you.

4. Keep Learning

Try something new or rediscover an old interest. Set a challenge that you will enjoy achieving. Learning new things helps you to become more confident as well as being fun.

5. Give

Do something nice for a friend, remember to say 'thanks' and smile. Seeing yourself as belonging to a wider community is very rewarding and helps to create new connections with people (see point one).

www.nef.org

Part Three

Lesson Materials: Sometimes My Brain Hurts

Introduction

There are three main themes to be covered:

1. What is mental health and mental illness?
2. What helps and what does not?
3. Why is mental health important?

Each of the three themes begins with a summary that allows the reader to become familiar with the content and background information needed to teach the lessons.

These lesson plans cover a range of subjects relating to mental health education. The following topics are covered:

- What is mental health?
- What goes wrong?
- What is mental illness?
- Stigma and discrimination.
- What helps?
- Language.
- Mental health promotion.
- Media portrayal.
- Risk and resilience.

All lesson plans are set in the following format:

- Introduction.
- Resources.
- Aims relating to what the children should achieve from the lesson with information on suitable discussion points.
- The method of the lesson plan, how to introduce the subject and proceed with the lesson. Additional teacher notes are included.

Each session should start with a reminder of the ground rules. A variety of activities accompany the lesson plans along with activity pages for children to complete. Each Key Stage 2 year group has two lesson plans for each theme and this can be incorporated in a way to suit the school timetable. The programme compliments the key elements within the SEAL material.

The idea is that from Years 3 to 6 all pupils receive age-appropriate mental health information throughout the school years.

Aims and Objectives for the Programme

Sometimes My Brain Hurts

The following aims and objectives apply to the programme and as you modify the sessions to meet the needs of the young people, the aims and objectives will change accordingly. While there are many similarities between establishments, there are also particular considerations and therefore, additional aims and objectives could be incorporated. Alternatively, some could be deleted or amended accordingly as the teacher deems appropriate.

Examples of aims and objectives:

- To develop sensitivity towards the needs of others.
- To educate against discrimination and prejudice.
- To empower children to make informed choices.
- To create a better understanding of mental health.
- To raise awareness of mental ill health issues.
- To explore what promotes positive mental health.
- To examine what impacts in a negative way.
- To identify stigma.
- To challenge derogatory language.
- To understand how early identification and interventions help.
- To provide opportunities for discussion.
- To protect children from inappropriate media portrayal of mental health problems.

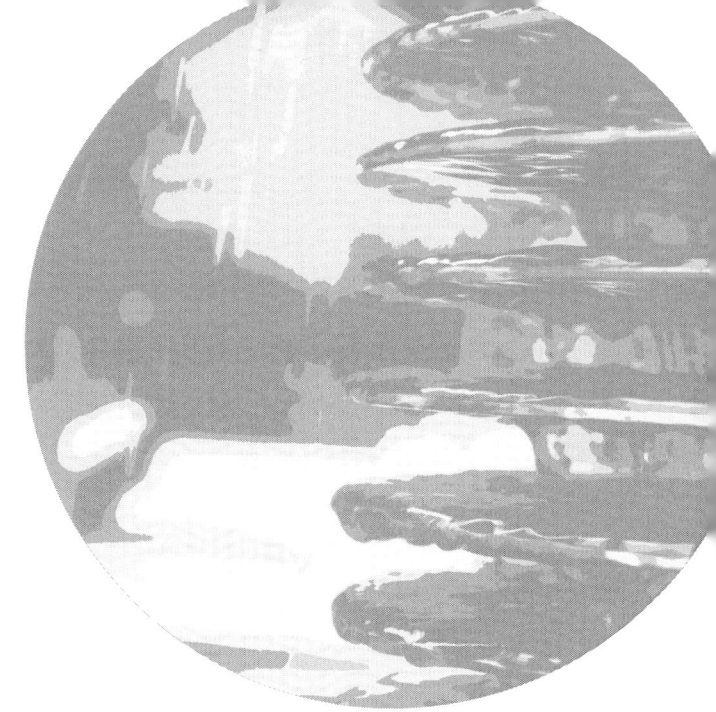

Year 3

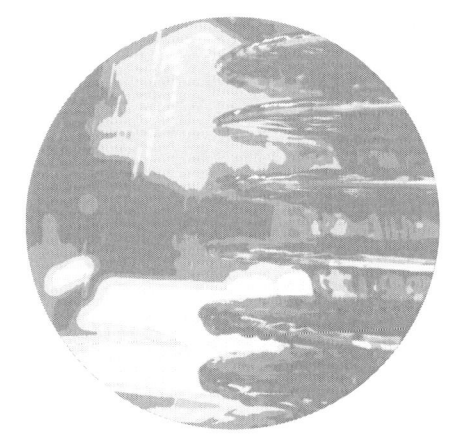

Summary

Summary

The language of mental health itself causes concern as many people's interpretation of the word mental is in relation to illness. When asked what their understanding of mental health is, many individuals, regardless of age, respond by naming mental health disorders such as depression or schizophrenia. Everyone has mental health and the fact that it does not get talked about contributes to the stigma and discrimination. It is interesting to note that psychosis is more common than diabetes, however, while most of us know a person with diabetes, how many of us know a person with psychosis? The only explanation for this is that within our society it is perfectly acceptable to disclose a condition such as diabetes along with many other physical health conditions, while it does not sit comfortably with people when someone shares that they experience panic attacks or extreme anxiety.

Comparisons may be made with sexual health, another subject that leaves some people feeling very uncomfortable. It could be argued that if we do not talk to children and young people about these topics, their confusion and misunderstanding will continue. There is a real opportunity to explore the subject of mental health with children at Key Stage 2 when many of them will not have formed negative viewpoints and prejudice.

There is a wealth of evidence to suggest that early intervention prevents mental health problems from getting worse. The National Health Service (2011) has funded an initiative called *Improving Access to Psychological Therapies* following extensive research into this topic (http://www.dh.gov.uk/en/Publicationsandstatistics/Publications/ PublicationsPolicyAndGuidance/DH_083150). However, many people, including young people, do not seek help and support for fear of being judged and also a belief that there is no help available. Therefore, if young people are more comfortable talking about mental health and have some knowledge of the subject, especially what helps and what does not, future problems might be considerably reduced.

The lesson plans contain opportunities for pupils to explore what impacts upon mental health, which in turn highlights strategies for improving mental health and wellbeing. Key messages such as how important it is to talk to someone when you are worried are revisited throughout the programme.

Many children in Year 3 will not have knowledge of mental health and the problems associated with it. It is probably safe to say that the majority will not have even given it any thought at all. This is an area that is to be explored and comparisons made with physical health. Children in primary schools are bombarded with messages about eating healthily and getting enough exercise and so on, however, they receive few messages about how to take care of their mental and emotional wellbeing.

The lesson aims for Year 3 are to explore their knowledge and increase their understanding and awareness through activities and discussion and through the creation of a folder that they can use for reference purposes in future classes.

Some important key messages for children in Year 3 are that recovery from mental illness is not only possible but likely and there are many avenues for help, support and guidance. They will also learn how helpful it is to talk about mental health and that people are very able to help themselves to get well.

Ground Rules Example

1. Be polite to all people.

2. Respect others' opinions.

3. Put your hand up if you want to speak.

4. Only one person speaks at a time.

5. You have the right to pass.

6. Listen to who is speaking.

7. Talk about yourself and let other people talk for themselves.

8. Be thoughtful and considerate at all times.

Many Year 3 pupils will not have heard the word 'confidentiality' or understand what it means, therefore it is a good idea to introduce it as part of the ground rules. This is quite difficult as the definition refers to speaking or writing in confidence, between us, classified, hush hush, private, off the record and secret, whereas many of the messages within the programme encourage children to talk about worries and concerns. It is important for the teacher to explain that talking about other people is not permitted within the lessons, and many of the suggested ground rules incorporate the essence of confidentiality.

Additional rules may be added or existing ones adapted to ensure that the group achieves ownership of the ground rules.

It is advisable to revisit the ground rules at the start of every lesson to enable pupils to feel safe and therefore able to contribute to discussions and activities and gain more from the sessions.

Theme One: What is Mental Health and Mental Illness?

Lesson 1: Comparisons with Physical Health

Introduction

By the end of the lesson all the pupils will have some understanding of what mental health is and appreciate that we all have mental health. Children in Year 3 will have some knowledge and understanding of physical health. For example, eating a healthy diet and getting regular exercise is good for them and helps them to grow and stay healthy. Therefore the initial sessions will focus upon physical health and make comparisons with mental health. Emphasis will be placed on how to take care of both.

Resources

- New folders entitled Sometimes My Brain Hurts.
- Front Cover for folders.
- Flipchart and pens or whiteboard.
- Range of coloured pens and paper.
- Comparison with Physical and Mental Health activity page.
- Word Search activity page.

Aims

- To gain some understanding of what is meant by the term mental health.
- For children to appreciate we all have mental health.
- To make some comparison with mental and physical health.

Method

Setting the Ground Rules

Introduce the session by developing a group agreement on ground rules to ensure that everybody feels safe. An example is included at the start of the section.

It might be that a pupil in the class has a member of their family who experiences mental health problems and this might make them feel uncomfortable discussing it. While most teachers are used to dealing with challenging subject matter, it is difficult to know what might be raised among the pupils in their class. It is advisable to have another member of staff in the classroom for these sessions, this could perhaps be a teaching assistant or learning mentor. The purpose of this is that if a pupil needs to take some 'time out' of the classroom if they are upset then they have the opportunity to have someone with them to offer comfort and the lesson can continue.

Starting the Session

The aim of the introductory session for Year 3 is to explore pupils' understanding of mental health. This session should be started with an open discussion where any ideas may be shared. The teacher introduces the subject of mental health and explains that in small groups pupils will explore their own understanding of what mental health and mental illness means to them. Pupils are asked for their first thoughts, impressions and feelings towards mental health. Useful prompts might be, 'What do I look like when I am well?' 'How would you describe good mental health?' General questions about health to promote discussion should be encouraged. Pupils are asked what being healthy means to them. The teacher can refer to the glossary for definitions and introduce some mental health terms and go on to explore how mental health is different from physical health.

Activities

Design a Front Cover for the Folder

The programme is called 'Sometimes My Brain Hurts' and this is the title to be used by pupils who are given new folders to complete. They will add to them during each session and start by designing the front cover. This should be a picture illustrating what mental health means to them. They will then have a resource they have created to refer back to. A front cover for pupils to create their own design can be found at the end of the session and printed from the CD-ROM.

Comparing Mental and Physical Health

Pupils are given the Comparisons with Physical and Mental Health activity page and asked to draw pictures. The teacher provides them with some suggestions such as a person exercising or eating fruit on the physical side. While for the mental health side they could show a person sitting on their own. They could also show expressions such as happy, smiling or sad. If the school group are familiar with the SEAL materials, this could be a useful reference point for them.

Word Search

The lesson ends with the Word Search activity page and pupils are encouraged to ask questions.

Discussion

The groups give feedback on their thoughts and ideas of what mental health is and the teacher facilitates the discussion highlighting the important point about the fact that we all have mental health. Reassurance should be given that at this stage there are no wrong answers just ideas to be explored as a starting point. The class can also share their pictures representing their idea of mental health.

Sometimes My Brain Hurts

Name:

Comparisons with Physical and Mental Health

Physical Health	Mental Health

Wordsearch

Find the following words in the grid:

happy	sad
bullying	childline
stress	healthy
mind	talk
grumpy	friends

e	y	s	c	t	t	t	t	u	s
n	a	t	g	a	i	a	f	s	p
i	d	r	n	n	m	l	r	u	m
l	h	e	i	p	e	k	i	a	e
d	e	s	y	f	s	n	e	n	d
l	a	s	l	g	s	a	n	e	n
i	l	n	l	a	a	t	d	o	i
h	t	a	u	t	e	t	s	t	m
c	h	a	b	g	r	u	m	p	y
s	y	t	r	h	a	p	p	y	p

Theme One: What is Mental Health and Mental Illness?

Lesson 2: Mental Illness

Introduction

Having brainstormed ideas of what mental health is and made comparisons with physical health, this session will introduce mental ill health. Using a gingerbread person, the class is asked to draw how the body is affected when both well and unwell and consider some mental health disorders.

Resources

- Folders entitled Sometimes My Brain Hurts.
- Range of coloured pens and paper.
- Gingerbread People activity page.

Aims

- To look more closely at what affects our physical and mental health.
- To be introduced to mental ill health and what that might look like.

Method

Starting the Session

At the start of each session the group rules should be revisited and added to if required. This is the opportunity for the teacher to ask questions, establish prior learning and clear up any outstanding concerns or misunderstandings. The class can then move on to the next activity.

Identifying Mental and Physical Ill Health

The teacher will need to provide suggestions for the class to consider, for example, if the brain has no oxygen it will not work and a person would become unconscious. Other factors affecting our mental wellbeing include becoming dehydrated and not having enough to eat. When we are dehydrated or our blood sugar level is low, it is difficult to concentrate and we may become very irritable or anxious. It is useful to revisit comparisons with physical health. Year 3 children will probably be familiar with conditions such as asthma or hay fever which many people experience. They may also be able to identify triggers for these conditions, such as pollen or pet hairs. In the same way there are triggers for poor mental health, such as bereavement or another form of loss, which might lead to depression or anxiety.

Activity

Pupils are given the Gingerbread People activity pages and asked to draw symptoms for physical and mental health. Positive signs of health would include a person out in the sunshine with friends being active with a smile on their face. They then draw how the body is affected when mentally or physically unwell. This will look quite different, the person will probably be on their own, maybe inside with an unhappy expression. Also, possibly, not looking as though they have bothered to wash or brush their hair, this can be illustrated on the gingerbread person with negative signs. A key message here is that mental ill health is more difficult to identify. The table below will provide a useful prompt for the teacher to ensure ideas that the class might not have thought of, are included and explored.

The teacher should make the distinction between feeling fed up and true depression. For example, everyone feels fed up and down sometimes. However, depression is when a person does not get any pleasure or enjoyment from things they used to and when the sense of hopelessness persists and prevents a person from doing things that they would choose to. They may also stop taking care of themselves and therefore their physical health becomes affected by the depression as illustrated by the gingerbread people.

The teacher can highlight that anxiety is normal and everyone feels anxious sometimes. Pupils are asked to give examples of what would make them nervous, such as competing in a sports or dance event. The teacher should emphasise that some stress can be helpful for us to perform at our optimum level. When trying new things it is natural to feel unsure, even a bit panicky but afterwards there can be a tremendous sense of achievement. Anxiety disorders, which will be explored in more detail in Year 4, exist when the level of panic prevents a person from functioning. The teacher provides an example such as obsessive compulsive disorder, when a person may have to make so many checks on whether lights are switched off, that they may not actually get to leave the house.

Physical Health Problems	Mental Health Problems
Colds, coughs and sore throats, pupils would draw a runny nose.	Feeling very low/depressed, indicated by a sad expression.
Broken bones, sprains or aches and pains, this might be illustrated on the Gingerbread People showing plaster cast.	Panic attacks and feeling very anxious or worried/unable to do things like go outside, perhaps butterflies in the stomach.
Asthma, eczema, hay fever and allergies.	Hearing voices or seeing things/ hallucinations.
Heart attacks or needing an operation.	Hurting yourself or not eating, cuts on Gingerbread's arm.

Discussion

When the Gingerbread People activity pages are completed, the teacher can take feedback and add to the suggestions of the class if they have forgotten anything. It should be pointed out to pupils that although it is relatively easy to see with our own eyes when a person is physically unwell, it is not always apparent when they have a mental illness. Individuals become very good at hiding their pain for fear of being judged.

Gingerbread People:
Positive Signs of Health

Gingerbread People: Negative Signs of Health

Theme Two: What Helps and What Does Not?

Lesson 1: Healthy Minds and Healthy Brains

Introduction

This session will focus on how to take care of your brain and your body, making links with exercise and feeling good. Discussion points include that while sunlight is good for you and promotes the production of Vitamin D within the body, it can also be harmful. Too much exposure to strong sun may cause skin to burn and may even lead to certain forms of skin cancer. The key comparison with mental health is that there is now a recognised condition called seasonal affective disorder that affects people during the winter months. It can lead to depression when certain individuals are deprived of adequate sunlight.

Resources

- Folders entitled Sometimes My Brain Hurts.
- Mental Health Collage activity page or large sheets of paper.
- Pictures from magazines to glue and stick on.
- Pens and crayons.

Aims

- For pupils to explore what impacts upon both our mental and physical health.
- To consider how different things affect different people.
- To gain some understanding that becoming mentally unwell is not a choice.
- By the end of the lesson pupils will have considered what helps to keep their brain healthy and what does not. Again the links are made between physical and mental health.

Method

Starting the Session

The group rules should be revisited and the teacher should check out any outstanding questions or issues from the earlier sessions. It is important to clear up any misunderstandings as they arise.

What Helps Mental Health and What Does Not?

The teacher leads a discussion on what helps mental health and what does not and provides the class with some ideas and suggestions. An example is having someone you can trust to talk to is helpful, while being alone and feeling afraid is not.

It is important to build on existing knowledge, and the teacher can introduce the idea of a trigger that might impact upon our physical health such as exposure to diseases and colds. They would then go on to highlight one that would harm our mental health such as being bullied which might lead to depression. Care must be taken, as it is highly likely a child in the class has had an experience of this, and referral to the group agreement again would help. Another example would be when a person is feeling very anxious or afraid it is possible to feel physical pain.

Activity

Creating a Collage

Magazines are distributed for the class to cut out pictures to illustrate mental health. Alternatively, they could draw how they would represent what helps and what does not directly into their folders on the activity page provided. An example of this could be a group of people together having fun and laughing to depict helpful, and conversely, a person alone and isolated, therefore not helpful. This lesson will try to show that although a person might be mentally unwell, they could appear perfectly fine to those around them and even be smiling. Pupils are encouraged to be creative and the collage should be colourful and eye catching, and convey messages about mental health in a very positive way. The completed pages could be displayed in the classroom and then added to the folders.

Discussion

When the class have completed the activity the teacher can take feedback, and the pupils will have the opportunity to share their ideas and present their suggestions. The teacher can offer additional suggestions on how to help promote good mental health and its importance. The lesson ends with questions.

Mental Health Collage:
Healthy Mind and Healthy Brains

What helps?	What does not?

Theme Two: What Helps and What Does Not?

Lesson 2: Finding Support

Introduction

This session will focus upon the importance of having good support from family and friends in order to promote positive mental health. Pupils will consider in more detail, some of the things they do that might impact in either a positive or negative way on their own emotional wellbeing. This will be achieved through discussion and completing the activity pages which will be added to their existing folders.

Resources

- Folders entitled Sometimes My Brain Hurts.
- Pens and crayons.
- Circle of Support activity page.
- Sally's Friends activity page.

Aims

- For pupils to understand how support from friends and family promotes positive mental health.
- By the end of the session pupils will have explored who they might turn to for advice.
- Pupils will have greater knowledge about how small things impact upon their mental health.

Method

Starting the Session

The group agreement should be revisited as with every session and the teacher should check out any outstanding questions or issues from the earlier sessions.

Finding Support

The teacher will outline the aims of the session for the children and emphasise the importance of support. Examples of how people have felt when they have shared a problem may be discussed to set the context. Also, being mindful to ensure the safety of pupils at all times, the teacher could ask for examples of when a person did not ask for help and what the outcome of that was.

Activities

Circle of Support

Pupils are asked to complete the Circle of Support page filling in each concentric circle, showing who they might talk to first to help them if they were worried or anxious about something, and then complete the outer circles with others who might be able to offer support. An example within the inner circle might be their parents/siblings, closely followed by friends, and after that might come teachers and doctors.

Sally's Friends

Pupils complete the maze to help Sally find her friends and this illustrates the importance again of having people you trust and who care about you.

Discussion

Following the activities, the teacher leads a discussion on how important it is to have friends and a support network around you to keep mentally and emotionally well.

Circle of Support

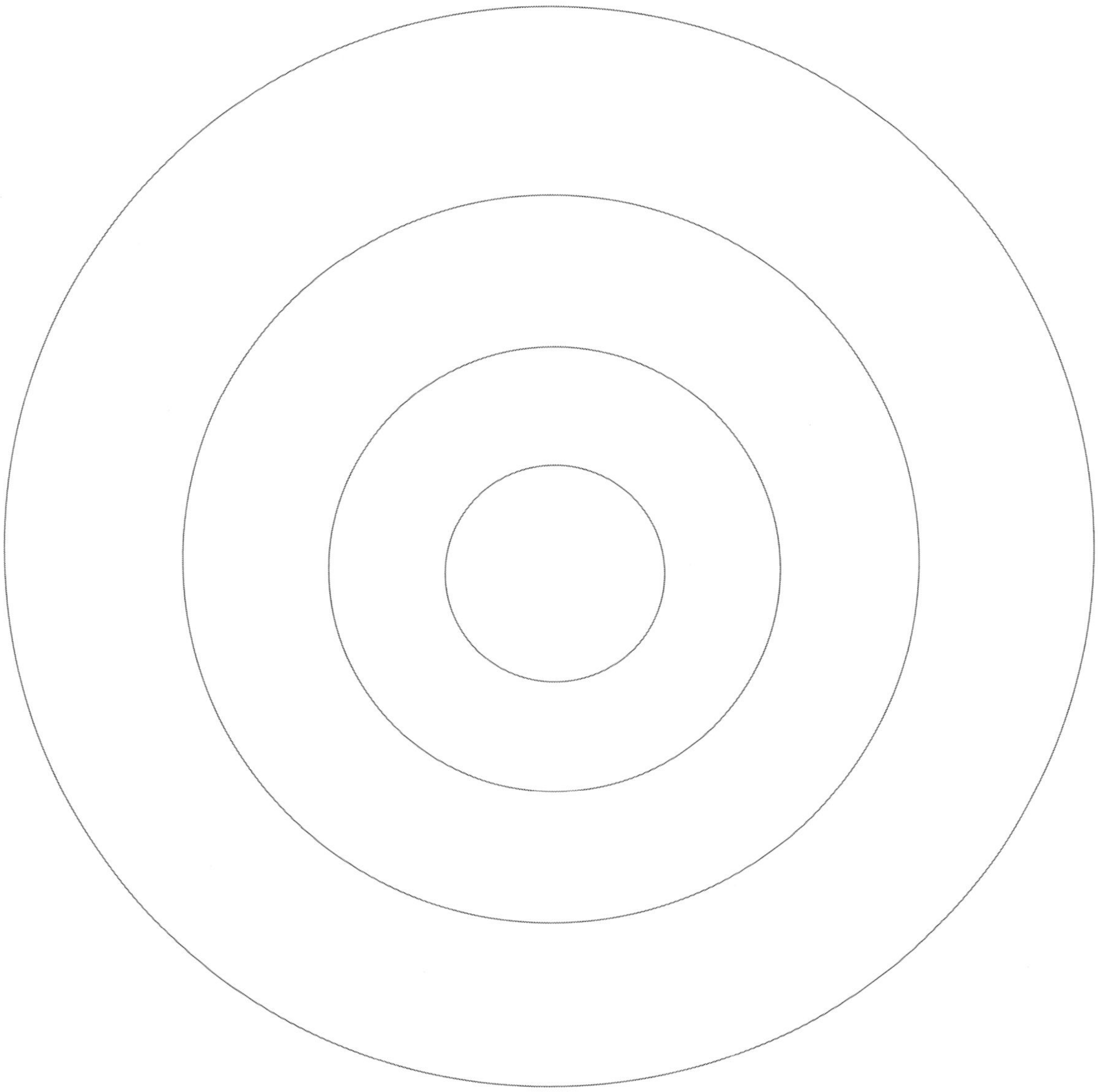

Put the names or draw pictures of people who can help to promote your positive mental health and keep you well. Draw a picture of yourself in the centre.

Sally's Friends

Can you help Sally to find her friends?
Sally really wants to join her friends on the other side of the maze.
Draw her path through the maze so that she can be with them.

Theme Three: Why is Mental Health Important?

Lesson 1: What Happens When You Become Unwell?

Introduction

The aim of this session is to get pupils thinking about accessing help for physical and mental health problems. They also need to consider how they might know they were unwell and what they might do about it. The information contained within this session builds upon the knowledge already acquired and emphasises how important it is to seek help early on, when the problem is developing, and has not become much bigger and therefore more difficult to deal with.

This session can introduce the stigma and discrimination associated with mental ill health and why seeking help is important, as well as ways to take care of your own mental health being emphasised and revisited. Pupils are asked what they know about physical health including where they get their information. They are also asked to question how accurate it is and how they know this for certain. What do they know about medicine and how safe it is? If you have a physical health problem, what happens, how, where and why? They are then asked to think about what they know regarding their mental health and apply the same questions.

Resources

- Sometimes My Brain Hurts folders.
- Pens and crayons.
- What Happens When You Become Unwell activity page.
- Alisha's Story activity page.

Aims

- By the end of the session pupils will have considered how they might recognise a mental health problem.
- They will have explored why people do not seek help with mental health problems.
- Stigma and discrimination will have been introduced.

Method

Starting the Session

As with all the previous sessions, pupils are reminded of the importance of the ground rules to ensure that everyone stays safe. The teacher will remind the class of previous discussions when comparisons were made with physical and mental health.

What Happens When You Become Unwell?

The teacher provides an example, if a child has a very bad cold they would almost immediately know they were unwell and speak to their parents or carers. The parents or carers would probably give their child some medication to relieve their symptoms, such as cough mixture for a bad cough. They, in turn, would take some action by explaining to the school that their child was unwell and unable to attend school until they felt better. They might also seek medical help if the child did not improve. Some bad colds develop into chest infections and require extra medication in the form of antibiotics. In extreme cases the child might have to be admitted to hospital in order for them to fully recover and this would all take some time. Nobody would expect the child to recover immediately from a serious physical health condition. The help would be sought almost as soon as the problem was identified and why would anyone not seek help when they felt unwell? Most people acknowledge when they are unwell and do something about it. However, the issue here is would it be the same for mental health problems?

There is a lot of evidence to suggest that not only do people not easily recognise when they are developing a mental health problem, they do not seek help. This session provides the teacher with an opportunity to explore why people might not seek help and introduces the idea of stigma and discrimination. Many people feel judged and also do not believe that there is really anything that can help them.

Activities

What Happens When You Become Unwell?

The teacher introduces the activity and gives examples regarding physical health problems and asks the class to give additional examples of their own which might include having to go to hospital with a broken bone and so on. They are then asked to complete the activity page in groups. How would they know if a person was mentally unwell and what might they look like?

Alisha's Story

The lesson will end with Alisha's story and the pupils are asked to consider at which points in the story Alisha might have been feeling really well, with factors that contributed to her mental and emotional wellbeing, and also the points at which she might have felt vulnerable. This provides the opportunity for the teacher to introduce the terms resilience and vulnerability, which will be explored in more detail with the Year 4 activities.

Discussion

The teacher will take feedback, facilitate discussion and answer any outstanding questions.

What Happens When You Become Unwell?

	Physical Health	Mental Health
How do you know?		
Who helps you with it?		
Where do you find them?		
How does help happen?		
When do you get help?		
Why do you get help?		

Alisha's Story

Alisha woke up and felt some warmth on her bed. As she stretched and yawned thinking it was time to get out of bed, she reached down and stroked her pet cat, Smartie. Smartie purred and nestled further into Alisha.

Mum yelled upstairs, 'I can't believe you are not up and dressed yet, for goodness sake hurry up.' 'Coming mum, don't stress,' called Alisha jumping up suddenly and tipping Smartie off the bed! The little cat glared, licked herself furiously for a few moments and then strutted out of the room with a momentary haughty glare at Alisha. 'Oh I'm sorry puss but you know what mum is like when she gets cross,' sighed Alisha wondering if her little brother had heard mum.

Alisha was eight years old and Ben was five and really just a baby. Mum didn't get so annoyed with Ben, but Alisha didn't mind as she loved her brother, especially when she made him laugh. Ben laughed a lot about nothing in particular and it was lovely to hear him. Mum didn't laugh very often especially since Dad left. When Alisha got downstairs Mum was lighting another cigarette! Alisha wished Mum wouldn't smoke. Apart from the fact that it made everything smell horrible she thought it might make Mum ill. She could even die!!

Mum gestured toward the cupboard where the cereals were kept. Alisha helped herself and got a bowl out for Ben but there wasn't enough milk for both of them so she tipped her Rice Krispies back into the box saying she didn't feel like any today. Mum shrugged and smiled at Ben as he tucked into his breakfast. 'Well at least have some juice,' she suggested to Alisha. 'No wait, I forgot to get any,' she finished before Alisha had a chance to respond. 'It doesn't matter Mum I need to get going anyway. Bye.' She tried to hug her mum but was waved away. 'Don't fuss,' said her mum, busy texting someone.

Alisha left the house and wandered along the road. She was about to head for Jenny's house when she remembered they had fallen out. She and Jenny had been friends since playgroup, but yesterday Jenny said that Alisha's mum was fat and lazy and no wonder her dad left. Alisha had rushed off feeling very angry and upset, how dare her friend say such cruel things, even if, and this was the part that hurt the most, there might be some truth in it.

Alisha arrived at school realising that she had forgotten her PE kit. Mrs Morgan would not be impressed as that happened last week as well. Alisha felt very low, like the sun had gone behind a cloud. She shivered slightly, pushed open the door to her classroom and planted a smile on her face.

When Mrs Morgan had called the register she asked everyone to change for PE. Alisha miserably moved towards her teacher's desk to explain but without looking up Mrs Morgan said, 'Don't waste time Alisha, go on and get ready.' 'But…' 'Go on now.' 'But…' 'Oh really, what is it now?' 'I haven't got my PE kit.' 'Why not?' 'I forgot.' 'Well that's the second time. I had better have a word with your mother.' 'Oh please don't, she's not well!' blurted Alisha, dreading the thought of Mrs Morgan coming around to the house and thinking that it would only make her mum cross. 'Very well, don't let it happen again. Ask someone in the class to see if they can help, I will see you later.'

Theme Three: Why is Mental Health Important?

Lesson 2: Language for Mental Health

Introduction

This final session for Year 3 pupils aims to reinforce some of the previous messages as well as building on their knowledge and understanding of mental health and wellbeing. As with previous sessions it is important to clear up any misunderstandings and answer questions as they arise.

Resources

- Sometimes My Brain Hurts folders.
- Pens and crayons.
- Language for Mental Health activity pages.
- Snakes and Ladders activity page.
- What I Have Learned About Mental Health activity page.
- Pupil Evaluation sheets.

Aims

- By the end of the lesson pupils will have explored some language associated with mental health.
- Pupils will have revisited previous messages regarding what is helpful for positive mental health.
- Increased knowledge and understanding of the myths associated with mental health will have been introduced.

Method

Starting the Session

As with all the previous sessions pupils are reminded of the importance of the ground rules to ensure everyone stays safe. The teacher then starts the lesson by asking pupils to reflect on their learning over the previous lesson and identifies key messages and learning points. The teacher goes on to explain that this lesson revisits some of these points and aims to consolidate the pupils' learning. It is also a final opportunity to ask questions and share thoughts and ideas.

Activities

Language for Mental Health

The teacher distributes the Language for Mental Health activity page. Before the pupils start to complete the activity the teacher checks if everyone understands the words they are trying to place in the sentences.

When the pupils have completed the page, they are encouraged to share their answers and explore the meaning behind them in more detail.

The teacher asks individual pupils to read out their answers and explain why they placed the words in the gaps. For example, question seven refers to bullying and how it is cruel and can make people very unhappy, the teacher should ask for examples of how bullying occurs, the impact of it and how it could be tackled. This helps the lesson echo important messages from other lessons as well as expanding pupils' knowledge, understanding and context for mental health. A key message is that many everyday occurrences impact upon everyone's mental health and this will encourage pupils to be mindful of their actions towards one another. This idea also features within the SEAL material, which again adds to the comprehensive aspect of having important facts reinforced across the curriculum.

Snakes and Ladders

The lesson ends with the pupils playing the snakes and ladders game which emphasises the things that they can do to support their own mental and emotional wellbeing. This provides the teacher with another opportunity to highlight the importance of talking to someone when you are worried and taking care of your physical health, which impacts upon your mental and emotional wellbeing.

Discussion

The teacher facilitates a discussion and finishes by asking each pupil to complete the activity page What I Have Learned About Mental Health. The pupils are then asked to complete the evaluation for Year 3.

Language for Mental Health

Complete the sentences with words taken from the following list:

mental health, seasonal affective disorder, anxiety, talk, eating, unhappy, mental, hallucination, trust, unwell, dangerous, problem, helps, stress, choice, mostly.

1. We all need someone we can _ _ _ _ _.

2. Everyone has _ _ _ _ _ _ _ _ _ _ _ _.

3. If you _ _ _ _ to a person when you are worried it _ _ _ _ _.

4. Exercise is good for _ _ _ _ _ _ health too.

5. You can see if a person is physically _ _ _ _ _ _.

6. When a person is mentally unwell _ _ _ _ _ _ they will get better.

7. Bullying is cruel and can make people very _ _ _ _ _ _ _.

8. _ _ _ _ _ _ _ is when a person worries so much it prevents them doing what they want to.

9. Boys and girls can both have an _ _ _ _ _ _ disorder.

10. If a person sees, hears or smells some things that are not really there it is known as a _ _ _ _ _ _ _ _ _ _ _ .

11. People with mental health problems are not _ _ _ _ _ _ _ _ _.

12. I in 4 people will have a mental health _ _ _ _ _ _ _.

13. Some _ _ _ _ _ _ is helpful.

14. Depression is not a _ _ _ _ _ _.

15. When a person feels very low in the winter it is called _ .

Language for Mental Health Answers

1. We all need someone we can **trust**.

2. Everyone has **mental health**.

3. If you **talk** to a person when you are worried it **helps**.

4. Exercise is good for **mental** health too.

5. You can see if a person is physically **unwell**.

6. When a person is mentally unwell **mostly** they will get better.

7. Bullying is cruel and can make people very **unhappy**.

8. **Anxiety** is when a person worries so much it prevents them doing what they want to.

9. Boys and girls can both have an **eating** disorder.

10. If a person sees, hears or smells some things that are not really there it is known as a **hallucination**.

11. People with mental health problems are not **dangerous**.

12. 1 in 4 people will have a mental health **problem**.

13. Some **stress** is helpful.

14. Depression is not a **choice**.

15. When a person feels very low in the winter it is called **seasonal affective disorder**.

Snakes and Ladders

40	39	38	Was cruel to someone 37	36	35	34	33
25	26	27	28	Didn't show any interest in anything 29	30	31	Met with friends 32
24	23	Didn't talk about worries 22	21	20	19	18	Stayed in bed in the dark all day 17
Laughed a lot 9	10	11	Helped a friend 12	13	Didn't drink enough water 14	15	16
8	7	6	5	Did some exercise 4	3	2	1

What I Have Learned About Mental Health

1.

2.

3.

What can I do with this knowledge?

Year 3 Pupil Evaluation

1.	Did the lessons in the programme help you to understand a little bit more about mental health? Yes No
2.	Which session did you prefer most? Please explain why.
3.	Please tick all the subjects you have learned about: • Comparing mental health and physical health. • Identifying mental and physical ill health. • Healthy minds and healthy brains. • Finding support. • What happens when you become unwell? • Language for mental health.
4.	Is there anything else you would like to learn but did not cover in this programme?

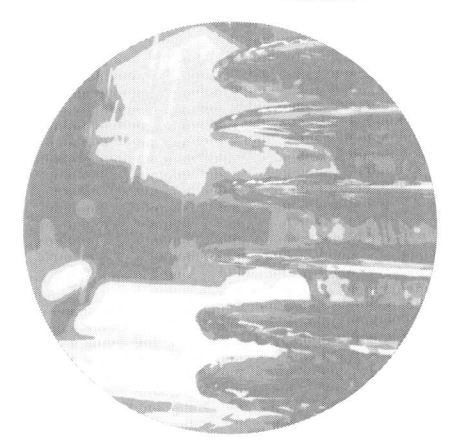

Year 4

Summary

Summary

The aim of this programme is to enable teachers and support staff within schools to talk to children about mental health and explore their knowledge and understanding. It will also convey important messages about how children can learn to take care of their mental health in the way that they learn to take care of physical health.

> Children with eating problems rarely approach services themselves, so families, friends and teachers are important in identifying a difficulty and then encouraging the young person to seek help.

(Bailey and Shooter, 2009)

These sessions will introduce some of the mental health conditions and encourage pupils to develop the correct language to use, including some definitions. The vast majority of people can identify with one of the most common mental health disorders because at some stage in their lives everyone experiences anxiety. Anxiety is a natural response and can be helpful in some situations where it prevents us from danger or motivates us to solve a problem. It can also become a problem and develop into a disabling disorder. If you consider people who compete in sports events or those who perform in the theatre, some level of anxiety will ensure that they achieve their optimum performance. However, the reverse of that is when the anxiety becomes so severe it actually prevents a person from living the sort of life they would wish to. Anxiety can vary in severity from a sense of mild unease to a terrifying panic attack, it can also last anything from a few moments to several years. It is the level of severity and duration that determine if it is a serious problem or not.

There is much evidence to suggest that early intervention can prevent mental health problems from getting worse. Young people who have experienced psychosis and had suicidal thoughts, report that the support of family and friends was the most helpful thing that aided their recovery. These sessions will draw together all the strands that have been examined so far. As with many new topics for pupils, it is useful to revisit prior knowledge and check out understanding. This is particularly true when discussing mental health, as it is not only the knowledge but the attitudes and values attached to the subject that are very important and need emphasising. Many people who have mental health disorders feel judged. The stigma and prejudice associated with mental ill health is embedded within our medicalised western society, and if you add fear and ignorance into the equation it does not help people who are distressed. Therefore, it could be argued that if younger children are educated about mental health problems they will realise a number of things including why people do not disclose mental health conditions or seek help. They will also understand what might help and how they can take care of their own mental and emotional wellbeing.

Ground Rules Example

1. Be polite to all people.

2. Respect others' opinions.

3. Put your hand up if you want to speak.

4. Only one person speaks at a time.

5. You have the right to pass.

6. Listen to who is speaking.

7. Talk about yourself and let other people talk for themselves.

8. Be thoughtful and considerate at all times.

Many Year 4 pupils will not have heard the word 'confidentiality' or understand what it means, therefore it is a good idea to introduce it as part of the ground rules. This is quite difficult as the definition refers to speaking or writing in confidence, between us, classified, hush hush, private, off the record and secret, whereas many of the messages within the programme encourage children to talk about worries and concerns. It is important for the teacher to explain that talking about other people is not permitted within the lessons, and many of the suggested ground rules incorporate the essence of confidentiality.

Additional rules may be added or existing ones adapted to ensure that the group achieves ownership of the ground rules.

It is advisable to revisit the ground rules at the start of every lesson to enable pupils to feel safe and therefore able to contribute to discussions and activities and gain more from the sessions.

Theme One: What is Mental Health and Mental Illness?

Lesson 1: Mental Health Continuum

Introduction

This session will build on the previous sessions from Year 3 and aims to establish greater understanding of mental health. Pupils are asked to reflect and discuss if their views and understanding of mental health have changed now that they are a year older and in a different class. Any questions that arise could be dealt with at this stage before going on to the next level. Pupils are also encouraged to write down questions as they occur. A question and discussion session can then be facilitated by the teacher at the end of the lesson.

Resources

- Folders from Year 3 entitled Sometimes My Brain Hurts.
- Flipchart and pens or whiteboard.
- Range of coloured pens and paper.
- Mental Health Continuum activity pages.

Aims

- To appreciate that we all have mental health.
- To be introduced to the idea of mental health on a continuum.
- To understand all sorts of factors and events that affect our mental health and wellbeing.

Method

Setting the Ground Rules

Introduce the session by developing a group agreement on ground rules to ensure that everybody feels safe, an example is included at the start of the section.

It might be that a pupil in the class has a member of their family who experiences mental health problems and this might make them feel uncomfortable discussing it. While most teachers are used to dealing with challenging subject matter, it is difficult to know what might be raised among the pupils in their class. It is advisable to have another member of staff in the classroom for these sessions, perhaps a teaching assistant or learning mentor. The purpose of this is that if a pupil needs to take some 'time out' of the classroom, if they are upset, they have the opportunity to have someone with them to offer comfort, and the lesson can continue.

Starting the Session

The purpose of this activity is to open up the idea of mental health on a continuum. The teacher should prepare the page with the words 'resilient' and 'vulnerable'. If there is access to a laminator this is helpful so that they can be used again. The words for the continuum may also be enlarged and laminated. Blank cards for the pupils to add their own suggestions will also be required.

Activities

Mental Health Continuum

Pupils are introduced to the idea of mental health on a continuum. This builds upon the idea that we all have mental health and it can be affected by many circumstances. At one end of the continuum is a person who is resilient and well both mentally and emotionally. This person is able to cope with the difficulties that life throws at them. At the other end is a vulnerable person who cannot cope with problems and is unwell.

Pupils are given a card with a word that relates to mental and emotional wellbeing. They are asked to stand on the continuum to indicate where they would be, either resilient or vulnerable, or anything else in between. Pupils are reminded that they can move up and down the continuum between resilient and vulnerable. They are also asked to make up their own words and situations that might move them along the continuum. Sometimes a big shift can happen during a school day. For example, the word 'sulking' would move you towards the vulnerable end but it is much more positive for your emotional wellbeing to talk about worries rather than bottle them up and dwell on them as they can become much bigger in your mind. An example of a resilient word would be 'encouraging'. There is evidence from research into positive psychology that doing something nice for another person actually enhances our own wellbeing.

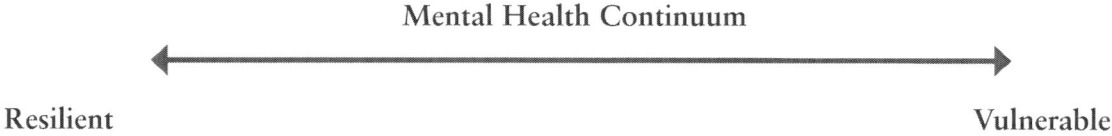

Mental Health Continuum

Resilient   Vulnerable

Discussion

Following the activity, pupils are asked to swap cards and repeat, if time allows, in order to explore different perspectives. The teacher then facilitates a discussion to highlight that mental and emotional wellbeing is not static, it is affected by many factors. The teacher should provide some examples to get the pupils started. These could include isolation, which affects mental and emotional wellbeing by making individuals more vulnerable. If you ask people of almost any age group what makes them happy, it is spending time with their family, friends and people who matter to them. There has been research into longevity and one of the common factors is connectivity; it is scientifically proven that if people feel involved, connected and cared about, they thrive. Having explored a sense of belonging, another example of positive regard could be discussed. Again, there is research to show that individuals thrive as long as they have one person who provides them with unconditional positive regard, and they will be even stronger and more fortunate if they have love.

Pupils are encouraged to think of as many words that relate to wellbeing as they can and write a list of them in their folders on the activity page. It is important to emphasise that there are positive as well as negative factors that affect mental and emotional wellbeing. It is easy to fall into a trap of focusing purely upon the negative aspects without realising that good things lift mood just as effectively as bad things lower it. This also re-enforces the message around recovery and helps pupils to accept that they cannot expect to feel well and happy all of the time, we all have down days and part of the programme is to look at ways in which to cope with those, as they cannot be avoided altogether.

Resilient

Vulnerable

Mental Health Continuum Words

Laughing	Walking
Crying	Watching
Singing	Hiding
Shouting	Arguing
Searching	Talking
Worrying	Planning
Listening	Showing Off
Pushing	Avoiding
Being Quiet	Dancing
Bullying	Praising
Hugging	Punishing
Ignoring	Questioning
Running	Being Active
Criticising	Complimenting
Writing	Resting

Mental Health Continuum Words

List as many words as you can that relate to wellbeing.

Positive	Negative

Theme One: What is Mental Health and Mental Illness?

Lesson 2: Signs and Symptoms of Mental Illness

Introduction

Pupils are asked to think of a time when they have felt worried or anxious. How did that feel and what did it look like? What was going on for them at that time? Each pupil is asked to think of a time when they felt sad or mad or unhappy, worried or angry and a variety of other feelings that they can choose for themselves.

The pupils are then asked to describe their feelings and consider how they might know how someone else is feeling. They should consider if it is a natural emotion or issue that is causing that person a problem. For example, when might just being 'worried' become a real anxiety disorder? The teacher is to ask the class what they know of mental health problems and how they would know if someone was mentally unwell. How can you tell if a person has a mental health problem, what does it look like and how do they act?

Resources

- Folders entitled Sometimes My Brain Hurts.
- Range of coloured pens and Blu-Tack.
- Mental Health Condition activity pages.
- Signs and Symptoms activity pages.

Aims

- For pupils to explore some of the mental health disorders.
- To learn the correct terms for some mental health disorders.
- To identify some of the signs and symptoms associated with mental ill health.

Method

Starting the Session

As with previous sessions the ground rules should be revisited and any outstanding questions or issues addressed before continuing on to the next exercise.

The teacher will need to make copies of the Mental Health Condition pages and also the Signs and Symptoms page that follows. As with previous exercises it is useful to enlarge them and laminate if possible. There is an additional sheet for the teacher to refer to, highlighting which signs and symptoms fit under which headings. It should be remembered that many of them will overlap and not just fit into one category. There are some additional signs and symptoms and this list is not exhaustive. Mental illness is very complex and more often than not a person will be experiencing two conditions. The most common is depression and anxiety, which often coexist, this is known as co-morbidity and makes diagnosis very difficult even for experienced clinicians.

Activity

Signs and Symptoms of Mental Illness

The teacher will introduce some of the mental ill health terms including depression, anxiety, psychosis and self-harm. The teacher then places the prepared pieces of paper with those terms on in each corner of the classroom.

Pupils are given the statements or words on cards and asked to place them under the heading in each corner. The idea is that pupils will gain understanding of what a person with each particular condition is experiencing and become familiar with signs and symptoms.

Discussion

The teacher facilitates a discussion to check out pupils' knowledge and understanding. This could start by asking how many of the terms were completely new for each pupil. Did they know of the language and what the conditions looked like?

Pupils are asked to consider how many of the signs and symptoms overlapped and how this contributes to misunderstandings and misdiagnosis. Pupils are then asked to name any other terms they have heard of relating to mental illness, such as bipolar disorder, schizophrenia or obsessive compulsive disorder.

Mental Health Conditions

Psychosis

Depression

Mental Health Conditions

Anxiety

Self-Harm

Signs and Symptoms of Mental Illness

Loss of appetite.	Feeling very worried.
Over-eating.	Sweating.
Difficulty sleeping.	Heart racing.
Sleeping too much.	Getting angry very quickly.
Crying.	Avoiding situations.
Very low mood.	Panicking.
Not enjoying anything.	Feeling sick.
Hearing voices.	Hurting yourself.
Seeing things that are not there.	Cutting yourself.
Thinking everyone is against you.	Not eating.
Losing touch with reality.	Making yourself sick.
Feeling that things are slowed down or speeded up.	Exercising excessively.
Staying in all the time.	Putting yourself down all the time.
Loss of memory.	

Teacher Notes: Signs and Symptoms of Mental Illness

Anxiety	Self-Harm
• Sweating. • Heart racing. • Getting angry very quickly. • Avoiding situations. • Panicking. • Feeling sick. • Repetitive behaviour. • Excessive hand washing. • Passing out. • Paranoia.	• Hurting yourself. • Cutting yourself. • Not eating. • Making yourself sick. • Exercising excessively. • Putting yourself down all the time. • Taking extreme risks. • Abusing substances including alcohol. • Smoking. • Pulling hair out.
Psychosis	Depression
• Hearing voices. • Seeing things that are not there. • Thinking everyone is against you. • Losing touch with reality. • Feeling that things are slowed down or speeded up. • Lack of self-care. • Extreme highs or lows.	• Loss of appetite. • Overeating. • Difficulty sleeping. • Sleeping too much. • Crying. • Very low mood. • Not enjoying anything. • Not seeing anyone. • Not going out. • Not talking to anyone. • Not taking care of yourself.

Theme Two: What Helps and What Does Not?

Lesson 1: Who Provides Support?

Introduction

This is an important session as research shows that many young people don't think they can ask for help, even if they acknowledge there is a problem. They don't always think that there is someone to help them or that anybody could make a difference. It is also an opportunity to introduce stigma and discrimination during discussion on why people might not ask for help.

Pupils are asked to consider who can help them to stay healthy. The list could include doctors and hospitals as well as friends and family. It is useful to highlight that for improvement of mental health, one of the most important factors is having someone they trust to talk to. People who are mentally unwell don't always need a therapeutic intervention such as counselling or medication.

Pupils are asked to consider who could help them if they were worried or anxious. How do they access support and help when in difficulties, what sort of language do they use?

Resources

- Sometimes My Brain Hurts folders.
- Pens and paper.
- Who Provides Support activity page.

Aims

- To gain understanding of people who might be able to offer support with mental wellbeing.
- Pupils will explore what might stop a person from asking for help.

Method

Starting the Session

Ground rules are revisited as with previous sessions. The teacher prepares enough diamonds for each group to complete the Who Provides Support? activity. These may be enlarged and laminated with spare ones for the pupils to be creative and write some of their own suggestions, which might be more specific to them.

Ask the class to think about who can help when they have a problem that is worrying them and making them anxious. What order should they approach them in, according to the severity of the problem? The teacher could provide an example of their own, perhaps if something was worrying them that related to a school situation. It would not be the most helpful subject to discuss with a family member as they would not fully appreciate or understand the whole picture and specific factors.

Sometimes it is useful to talk to a person who is outside and not involved, and sometimes it is not. Also pupils are asked to consider what makes a situation very serious, this might be something that requires medical intervention.

Activity

Who Provides Support?

A diamond nine exercise may be used to encourage discussion within groups. As with many of the exercises examining what helps for mental health problems, there are no absolute right or wrong answers and much of the discussion will focus upon individual preferences, attitudes and experience. The pupils are asked to think which order they would arrange the diamonds in to fit with their particular needs or requirements. This might vary considerably depending upon the issues that are concerning them at the time. For example, if something is not going well at school it might be more helpful to talk to the teacher rather than a doctor.

Each of the diamonds has a suggestion of people who can help and there is a blank one for pupils to suggest their own examples. The diamonds include a parent or carer, teacher and doctor. The idea is that they are arranged in order of preference. This will vary according to the individual and there is no absolutely correct answer.

Discussion

Pupils are asked to consider who can help them to stay healthy. They can then go on to discuss how people help each other and practise ways of asking for help. By the end of the session pupils will have had the opportunity to explore the various ways in which people can help them to stay healthy both physically and mentally, as well as considering ways in which they can take care of their own mental health.

Who Provides Support?

Parents or Carers

The Internet

Teachers

Doctor

Samaritans

Friends

Other Family Members

Self-Help Books

Theme Two: What Helps and What Does Not?

Lesson 2: Language for Mental Health

Introduction

This session will specifically focus upon the language associated with mental health. It will build upon existing knowledge and emphasise that there are correct terms, as well as derogatory ones.

Resources

- Sometimes My Brain Hurts folders.
- Pens and paper.
- Language for Mental Health activity pages.

Aims

- For pupils to be introduced to language associated with mental health.
- To explore in more detail some of the stigma and discrimination associated with mental health.

Method

Starting the Session

Ground rules are highlighted as this particular session might encourage some cruel terms and remarks so care should be taken to ensure that everyone feels safe. The teacher will need to print copies of the activity pages for pupils to add to their folders.

Activity

Language of Mental Health

The teacher issues the activity pages and asks the pupils to complete the correct and incorrect terms activity page when the words are read out. It might be necessary to refer to the glossary of terms and the teacher should provide some examples such as emotionally stable, coping, resilient, depression, anxiety, fear, stigma, for correct answers and for incorrect answers, some examples such as weirdo, mad, mental and dangerous. Pupils are given permission to be rude when adding additional incorrect terms to the page. They are also encouraged to think of as many correct and positive terms as they are able.

Discussion

When the pupils have completed the activity page and exhausted their lists, the teacher asks for feedback. Pupils should be encouraged to share where they have heard the language and how it makes them feel when using it. They are also asked to make comparisons with how many words are on each of their lists. Was it easier to think of additional incorrect words and why might that be the case? Is it easier to talk in negative terms and do people choose not to say anything if they are not sure what is correct?

Pupils are encouraged to consider, that if the incorrect terms are used to a person who is experiencing a mental health problem, what the effect will be on that individual. The teacher should highlight the extra distress that this may cause a person, also the far reaching effects upon their ability to recover and the ongoing discrimination they may encounter.

The teacher should highlight that the use of language is very important when avoiding the labelling of people. An example of this is to describe a person who lives with depression rather than calling them a depressive.

The pupils should place their completed activity pages in their folders. They can refer back to them and add to the lists as their knowledge increases. The pages will serve as a reminder of how they have extended their understanding, on completion of the programme.

Teacher Notes: Language for Mental Health

Correct Terms	Incorrect Terms
Worried	Nutter
Depression	Psycho
Anxious	Looney
Unwell	Sick
Psychosis	Weirdo
Emotional	Sado
Schizophrenia	Schizo
In Recovery	Mental
Stressed	Bonkers
Panicking	Mad
Unable to Cope	Useless
Needing Support	Pathetic
Vulnerable	Lazy
Unhappy	Thick
Sad	Weak

Language for Mental Health

Correct Terms	Incorrect Terms

Theme Three: Why is Mental Health Important?

Lesson 1: Promoting Positive Mental Health

Introduction

Pupils are encouraged to think about how to take care of their mental health in the future.

This session aims to encourage pupils to reflect upon what they have learned so far and create a poster to promote positive mental health. The teacher starts the session by asking for feedback on what helps, providing examples of having someone to talk to, getting enough sleep, exercise and so on. The teacher highlights the discussion around stigma and how sometimes mental health issues are regarded in a negative light.

Resources

- Sometimes My Brain Hurts folders.
- Pens and paper.
- Magazines.
- Access to the Internet.
- Promoting Positive Mental Health poster.

Aims

- For pupils to be creative and use their existing knowledge and understanding.
- To consider how mental health may be promoted in a positive way.
- To challenge stigma and discrimination.

Method

Starting the Session

Ground rules to be highlighted and outstanding questions answered. The teacher provides the Promoting Positive Mental Health poster as well as coloured pens and perhaps pictures for pupils to cut out and add to their poster.

Activity

Promoting Positive Mental Health

There is evidence that early intervention works best, as problems can grow and become much worse. The idea behind this activity is that pupils are encouraged to present mental health in a positive light This in turn will encourage discussion and ensure that they realise that seeking help early will help to prevent a situation becoming worse and also speed up the road to recovery. The pupils are encouraged to work in pairs or small groups to share ideas.

Using magazines, the teacher should ask for examples of posters that pupils find appealing and eye catching, what is it they like about them? What encourages them to try something? How do advertising people convey their messages?

If time permits, the pupils could undertake some research in magazines or on the internet to determine how best to convey their positive messages around mental health.

Really important messages should be conveyed on the posters. A key issue is about recovery so while the pupils have drawn negative signs of poor mental health on the gingerbread people, they now need to consider what a person who has recovered from a mental illness might look like. This could be a bright picture of someone spending time with friends, smiling and looking as though they are enjoying themselves. Also as mental health problems affect so many people, another important message might be about how talking over worries is good for all of us. The poster could include some positive messages from people who have found talking helpful, where they got their help and support from, and also sign posting to avenues for support such as Childline.

Discussion

When the posters are completed, the teacher asks for feedback and the pupils talk through their ideas with the rest of the class. The completed pages are then added to their folders.

The teacher helps the pupils to identify common themes that have emerged from the posters. These will include the importance of having someone to talk to who really listens. This provides a good link with the next session, which focuses upon the importance of good listening skills.

Promoting Positive Mental Health Poster

Theme Three: Why is Mental Health Important?

Lesson 2: Listening Skills

Introduction

The focus of this session is upon the importance of good listening skills, something that is not taught or valued perhaps as much as it should be. Family and friends are better placed to provide support and everybody can develop their listening skills. It is not always necessary for people with mental health problems to access support from professionals. While it could be argued that qualifications and experience are important, the factor that makes the real difference is the connection between two people. As long as somebody listens and cares they will be helping the other individual towards their recovery.

Resources

- Sometimes My Brain Hurts folders.
- The Best Friend Called Julie story page.
- Examples of Good Listening Skills page.
- Evaluation page.

Aims

- For pupils to realise the importance of good listening.
- Practise of listening skills to show how effective it is.

Method

Starting the Session

Ground rules to be highlighted and outstanding questions answered. The teacher then reads the story, The Best Friend Called Julie, and asks pupils for their thoughts and reactions to it.

Activity

Listening Skills

Pupils are divided into groups of three. Pupil A will do the talking first, they may talk about anything, it does not have to be a problem unless they want it to be. The teacher could provide some examples such as a recent holiday or day out somewhere. The pupils could talk about a person they admire and why that is, they could talk about a special hobby or a new pet, anything they like. Pupil B will be the listener. They are encouraged to practise good listening skills such as those highlighted on the example sheet, not interrupting, sitting still, not making assumptions and so on, and the pupils are asked to suggest more of their own. Pupil C is the observer and will provide feedback to pupil B as to how effective their listening skills were. Did they fidget and appear uninterested in what pupil A was saying or did they appear really engaged and interested? Also at this time, pupil A can describe how it felt for them. Points for consideration are whether they felt they were truly being listened to, or was pupil B a bit distracted or preoccupied? The teacher can explain that it is sometimes difficult to listen intently to a person when you have something on your own mind. This again makes the point that talking about worries is helpful as they take up a lot of space in your head, so that you can't engage in what is being presented to you and you may miss out. The pupils then all swap around so that everyone has the chance to play each part.

It is important to be realistic over how long pupils of this age group can fully focus and sit still listening, therefore allocating a couple of minutes for talking and then feedback will probably achieve the best results and they will not become bored or distracted.

Discussion

Pupils are asked to reflect on a time when they asked for help. Who did they turn to and what was the outcome? Particular emphasis is placed on whether they felt they were listened to.

If time permits, pupils could write a short story of their own like The Best Friend Called Julie and this may be added to their folders. Finally, the pupils are asked to complete the evaluation form.

The Best Friend Called Julie

Nobody knew about May's mum. The doctors had asked her dad not to share the information with either of his daughters or his mother-in-law. They were all very close and so he had to bare the huge burden alone. Everyone thought Valerie would get better, they hoped she would, as anything else was unthinkable. She had been ill for two years, with visits into hospital on a number of occasions. There was some surgery at one point and cancer was never mentioned. She died after a long battle, essentially a young, healthy woman at the age of 35.

She left behind a distraught husband and two young daughters who were confused, shocked and feeling very lost. People didn't know what to say or do. Many said absolutely nothing and life carried on, which made May want to scream, 'My mum has died, will somebody please say something?' but they didn't.

Death is such a taboo subject. People say things like 'gone to sleep' or 'passed away'. Nobody said, 'She is dead and you will never see her again'. The reality is that there isn't anything anyone could say to make it better or worse. Just an acknowledgment that something so unbelievably sad has happened would have been nice, May thought.

Time went by, May wasn't sure how much, as the days seemed to blend together and they all felt empty without her mum. May kept herself busy looking after her much younger sister and assumed the mother role. Dad was a terrible cook! School didn't feel very meaningful, why work hard for exams when you are going to die anyway?

Julie and May had always been friends and became much closer when May's best friend Jane moved away, another loss but in a different way as they could still keep in touch and meet up or stay over at one another's houses occasionally. Julie asked proper questions like, 'What does it feel like?' and 'Do you want to talk about it?' May found Julie to be the best listener ever. She did need to talk about her mum, a lot. It was almost as if talking about her kept her close. May knew deep down that she was not coming back, but there was a slight doubt or hope that she might. May had not had a chance to say goodbye properly. Lots of grownups, grandparents and aunties and her dad had decided that she and her sister should not go to the funeral as it would be too upsetting. May wondered who it would be too upsetting for.

Gradually May realised that when she talked to Julie, they actually started to laugh again and talk about nothing in particular. Sometimes when they were together, Julie didn't say anything at all, she just let May talk and it was so very helpful for May to have a voice. She could cry or get angry and there were no consequences. Julie didn't tip toe around her or try to make everything 'OK' because clearly she couldn't. She just listened.

Examples of Good Listening Skills

1. Not interrupting.

2. Nodding.

3. Making mmm sounds to show that you are listening.

4. Making eye contact.

5. Sitting still and not fidgeting.

6. Using the persons words to show you understand.

7. Smiling gently with kind eyes to encourage them to continue.

8. Not making assumptions.

9. Asking relevant questions.

10. Not competing or telling your own story.

11.

12.

13.

14.

15.

Year 4 Pupil Evaluation

1.	Did the lessons in the programme help you to understand a little bit more about mental health? Yes No
2.	Which session did you prefer most? Please explain why.
3.	Please tick all the subjects you have learned about: • Mental Health Continuum. • Signs and Symptoms of Mental Illness. • Who provides support? • Language for Mental Health. • Promoting Positive Mental Health. • Listening Skills.
4.	Is there anything else you would like to learn but did not cover in this programme?

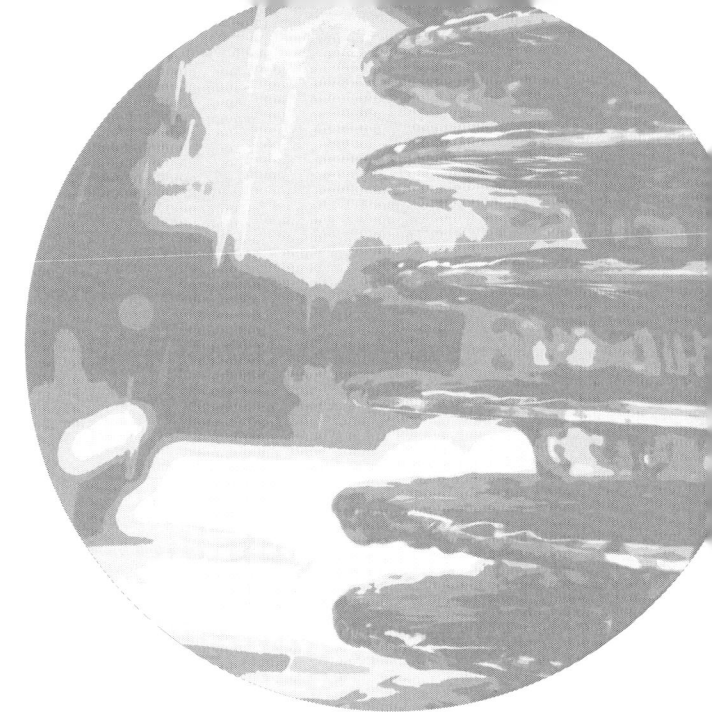

Year 5

Summary

Summary

The aim of the sessions for Year 5 pupils is to build upon the knowledge and understanding that they will already have gained from the sessions in Years 3 and 4.

> Today's primary school children face all kinds of challenges that threaten to derail them, from gang culture on our streets to abuse at home. Unless they are given the means to cope, their feelings of sadness, fear and anger can easily spill over in the classroom and in society and while some children may become disruptive, others will withdraw completely, shutting everyone out.

(Place2be, 2011)

Pupils are encouraged to ask questions and challenge some of the information presented to them. Theme One explores some of the risk and resilience factors that affect individual's mental and emotional wellbeing. Lesson 2 helps pupils to identify what is myth and what is reality. There is so much misunderstanding and ignorance on the subject of mental health, which helps to explain why people do not seek support in a timely manner.

Theme Two encourages pupils to be creative and consider what might make services for young people more accessible. They are also given scenarios to investigate and asked to provide solutions for particular problems presented to them. This is very empowering and enables the teacher to highlight that not all people with mental health problems need to access medical services. If they have the right support and someone who will listen to them among their friends and family, that might be all that is required to aid their recovery. Pupils will learn about how they could provide support for someone they care about, and also to identify some coping strategies of their own.

The final theme aims to extend and deepen knowledge and understanding of mental health problems through a quiz and some creative writing. Pupils are encouraged to discuss the activities and will hopefully be becoming more familiar with the correct terms to use. This in turn will reduce the fear experienced by many individuals when they come into contact with a person who is mentally distressed.

As with many of the other sessions in the programme the teacher is encouraged to challenge stigma and discrimination.

Ground Rules Example

1. Be polite to all people.
2. Respect others' opinions.
3. Put your hand up if you want to speak.
4. Only one person speaks at a time.
5. You have the right to pass.
6. Listen to who is speaking.
7. Talk about yourself and let other people talk for themselves.
8. Be thoughtful and considerate at all times.

Many Year 5 pupils will not have heard the word 'confidentiality' or understand what it means, therefore it is a good idea to introduce it as part of the ground rules. This is quite difficult as the definition refers to speaking or writing in confidence, between us, classified, hush hush, private, off the record and secret, whereas many of the messages within the programme encourage children to talk about worries and concerns. It is important for the teacher to explain that talking about other people is not permitted within the lessons, and many of the suggested ground rules incorporate the essence of confidentiality.

Additional rules may be added or existing ones adapted to ensure that the group achieves ownership of the ground rules.

It is advisable to revisit the ground rules at the start of every lesson to enable pupils to feel safe and therefore able to contribute to discussions and activities and gain more from the sessions.

Theme One: What is Mental Health and Mental Illness?

Lesson 1: Risk, Resilience and Mood States

Introduction

This session will build on the previous sessions from Years 3 and 4 and aims to establish greater understanding of mental health. Pupils are asked to reflect and discuss if their views and understanding of mental health has changed now they are a year older and in a different class. Pupils are encouraged to write down questions as they occur and a question and discussion session can then be facilitated by the teacher before going on to the next level.

Resources

- Folders from Year 3 and 4 entitled Sometimes My Brain Hurts.
- Flipchart and pens or whiteboard.
- Range of coloured pens and paper.
- Risk and Resilience Factors Cards.
- Risk and Resilience Factors activity pages.
- Mood States activity page.

Aims

- For pupils to realise that we all have mental health challenges and our moods vary according to what happens to us.
- To appreciate that what is helpful for one person might not be for another.

Method

Setting the Ground Rules

Introduce the session by developing a group agreement on the ground rules to ensure that everybody feels safe. An example is included at the start of the section. It is possible that a pupil in the class has a member of their family who experiences mental health problems and this might make them feel uncomfortable discussing it. While most teachers are used to dealing with challenging subject matter, it is difficult to know what might be raised among the pupils in their class. It is advisable to have another member of staff in the classroom for these sessions, this could perhaps be a teaching assistant or learning mentor. The purpose of this is that if a pupil needs to take some 'time out' of the classroom if they are upset, then they have the opportunity to have someone with them to offer comfort and the lesson can continue.

Starting the Session

The teacher should have prepared the Risk and Resilience Factors Cards by printing and enlarging them then laminating and cutting them up. A4 sheets with individual, family and community will need printing so that each group has a set. The lesson should be started by establishing with the pupils what their understanding of risk and resilience is. While most of the pupils will probably be familiar with what risk means, they might not understand resilience and one way in which the teacher can describe this is 'bouncebackability'. Basically, pupils need to understand about the ability to bounce back and pick themselves up when they have had a setback, disappointment or been hurt in some way.

Activities

Risk and Resilience

The teacher will produce the Risk and Resilience Factors on cards for the pupils and ask them to work in groups to explore the impact of what is said on the cards. They will continue their discussion by identifying which factors are associated with the individual, the family or the community. The pupils need to divide the risk and resilience factors between them. Each pupil can place their particular factor on the sheet they think most appropriate, either individual, family or community. The teacher will highlight for pupils that some of the factors may be placed under two or more headings. This again emphasises the complex nature of mental health and everything that impacts upon it.

Mood States

The teacher gives out the Mood State activity page and provides some examples for pupils. Elation might be represented when a pupil achieves something for themselves. This could be selection for a sports team, completing a piece of work or performing with a musical instrument. Feeling very low might be when there are constant arguments at home or if a pupil is unable to see a member of their family.

Discussion

When pupils have completed the Mood States activity page they are asked to provide feedback. This enables the teacher to facilitate a discussion on how lots of different circumstances impact upon individuals. Useful comparisons could be made to illustrate that we are all different and what will be meaningful for one person might not have resonance with another. This will also be a useful point to refer back to when pupils are being asked to consider what a service for young people would look like in Theme Two. The key message for improving mental health and emotional wellbeing is that one size does not fit all and it is important to have options.

Risk and Resilience Factors

Risk	Resilience
Poor nutrition.	A range of sporting or leisure activities.
Poor social coping skills.	At least one close relationship.
Gender conflict.	Good relationships with friends.
Exposure to drug misuse.	Sense of humour.
Emotional abuse.	Respect for authority.
Low self-esteem.	Being female.
Genetic influence.	Personal goals.
Oppressive, inconsistent or weak discipline.	Attending a successful school.
Hostile or rejecting relationships.	High self-esteem.
Violence in the community.	Involvement with an extended family.
A difficult temperament.	Good problem-solving skills.
Communication difficulties.	Secure early relationships.
Relative poverty.	Good housing.
Chronic illness.	Strong bonds within a family.
Being involved in a disaster.	A high income family.
Loss of a parent, relative or friend.	Taking part in community activities.
Physical or sexual abuse.	Others expressing high expectations.
Witnessing family conflict and violence.	Love and affection.
Discrimination and racism.	Good social skills.
Divorce and separation.	A positive attitude to life.
Family involvement in crime or drugs.	A stable environment.

Risk and Resilience Factors

Individual

Risk Factors	Resilience Factors

Risk and Resilience Factors

Family

Risk Factors	Resilience Factors

Risk and Resilience Factors

Community

Risk Factors	Resilience Factors

Mood States

Name:

A sense of elation (very excited):

....

....

A sense of heightened wellbeing:

....

....

Feeling well. What does this look like?

....

....

Feeling a bit down and unhappy. How would you know?

....

....

Feeling very low. What might have happened?

....

....

Theme One: What is Mental Health and Mental Illness?

Lesson 2: Myth or Reality

Introduction

Pupils will continue to develop their appreciation of what helps and what does not by working through some statements that the teacher will read out. There is a great deal of misunderstanding, stigma and prejudice associated with mental health and mental illness. This session will help pupils to explore some actual facts and increase their knowledge.

Resources

- Sometimes My Brain Hurts folders.
- Range of coloured pens and paper.
- Myth or Reality activity pages.

Aims

- To gain greater understanding of some of the myths associated with mental health and mental illness.
- To examine stigma and discrimination associated with mental illness.

Method

Starting the Session

Ground rules are highlighted and the teacher prepares the activity by printing the Myth or Reality statements for pupils to put in their folders. The answers to the activity are provided at the end of the lesson.

Activity

The session focuses on the issue of stigma and discrimination. Having printed the large sheets labelled Myth and Reality the teacher places them in opposite corners of the classroom.

The myth and reality statements are then read out by the teacher who asks the pupils to stand where they think the statement applies, either under the myth heading or reality. After the pupils have decided upon their positions, they are asked to explain their views and what has informed them. When the last statement has been read out and explored thoroughly, the teacher hands out the sheets so that the pupils have a copy for their folders. Pupils should be informed that this is not a test situation but an exercise to promote and encourage discussion and further exploration of the subject of mental health.

Discussion

The teacher facilitates a discussion as to why the pupils were standing in their chosen places. Pupils are asked to reflect upon their chosen positions and explore whether their views have changed having listened to the explanation and contributed to the discussion. This will help to build their understanding of stigma and discrimination as well as confirming their knowledge of mental ill health.

Mental Health Conditions

Myth

Reality

Reality or Myth

Statement	True or False
People with mental health problems are dangerous.	Myth
If you are mentally unwell or have a mental health problem, you will never recover.	Myth
Everyone can tell if you have a mental health problem.	Myth
There is always someone you can talk to about mental health.	Reality
Women have more mental health problems than men.	Reality
People who self-harm are attention seeking.	Myth
People who take their own lives are cowards.	Myth
1 in 10 young people between 5 and 15 years have mental health problems.	Reality
Schizophrenia is a serious illness with no cure.	Reality
Eating disorders are very common.	Myth
Depression only affects adults.	Myth
Panic attacks are like asthma attacks.	Reality

Myth or Reality Answers

Questions	Answers
People with mental health problems are dangerous.	Myth. The reality is that the person who is most likely to be harmed is the person with the mental health problem.
If you are mentally unwell or have a mental health problem, you will never recover.	Myth. There is extensive evidence that not only is it possible for people with mental health problems to recover, it is very likely.
Everyone can tell if you have a mental health problem.	Myth. Many mental health problems go unnoticed for years. This is partly due to people not recognising that they have a problem and partly because they do not seek help and support. It is also due to the fact that many people do not understand mental health problems.
There is always someone you can talk to about mental health.	Reality. This is true and sometimes it can be a friend or family member. It does not have to be a doctor or an expert in that area.
Women have more mental health problems than men.	Reality. Although this might be because women access support and talk about problems more readily than men.
People who self-harm are attention seeking.	Myth. Most self-harm is hidden and people describe it as a coping strategy. It is also worth noting that attention seeking is not always wrong, we all need attention at some stage and some people are better at asking for it than others.
People who take their own lives are cowards.	Myth. People who contemplate suicide are very unwell and cannot see another way to cope with their unbearable pain.
1 in 10 young people between 5 and 15 years have mental health problems.	Reality. This statistic is probably underestimated if anything, having highlighted that people do not recognise mental health problems or seek help. These figures relate to the young people who have accessed support through medical services.

Part 3: Year 5

Myth or Reality Answers (Cont)

Questions	Answers
Schizophrenia is a serious illness with no cure.	Reality. Schizophrenia is very serious and while there is effective treatment through medication and additional support through talking therapies, there is no actual cure.
Eating disorders are very common.	Myth. Eating disorders are relatively rare, although many people have emotional issues with food.
Depression only affects adults.	Myth. It was once believed that children and young people could not become depressed especially if there was no apparent reason. This is simply not true.
Panic attacks are like asthma attacks.	Reality. The two might become confused as they produce similar symptoms of struggling for breath.

Theme Two: What Helps and What Does Not?

Lesson 1: Problem Scenarios

Introduction

A key learning objective here is that there is not necessarily a one size fits all answer and there may be a number of solutions to any particular mental health problem. Pupils are encouraged to consider what they think might help a person in the situations provided on the scenario cards. This is where they are placed in the position of having the potential to help a friend and the idea is that they work in groups to discuss possible solutions for the problems outlined before them. They could also present their own ideas and problems that they may have heard of or made up.

Resources

- Sometimes My Brain Hurts folders.
- Scenario Cards activity page.
- Flipchart paper and pens.

Aims

- To gain understanding of how to help a person who is mentally unwell.
- For pupils to consider what helps and what does not using scenario cards.

Method

Starting the Session

Ground rules are re-established and the teacher divides the class up into groups. The teacher hands out the Scenario Cards that can be enlarged and laminated to ensure they are available for repeated use. Depending upon the time available, the teacher can decide whether to give each group every scenario or allocate certain problems for certain groups. One group could consider scenarios one, two and three, another group, numbers four to seven and the others, eight, nine and ten.

Activity

Scenarios

When the discussions have been completed, notes can be taken down by a group member so that they have a record of their solutions for the teacher to facilitate a discussion to share ideas.

This activity provides a safe way to discuss real scenarios without putting pupils in a difficult situation where they have to disclose their own issues. However, some of the scenarios may reflect what happens for many young people. If pupils wish to share some of their own issues the teacher should refer to the ground rules to ensure that everyone remains safe.

Discussion

When the teacher has taken all the feedback from the scenarios, pupils can be asked to consider any real life experiences and reflect on how they handled the situation at the time. Having completed the activity, pupils are asked to think about how they would act differently now with their increased knowledge and understanding. Would their advice and support for the scenarios before the lesson be different and if so in what way? This activity will illustrate to pupils how helpful unqualified people who care can be. The answers may be recorded and placed in the folders for future reference purposes.

Scenario Cards

1.	Your friend tells you that he has been feeling very low and nothing feels like it matters anymore. How do you feel and what would you do?
Group Solution	
2.	Your friend says that she is constantly worrying about all sorts of things, even little things that she knows don't matter. How do you feel and what would you do?
Group Solution	
3.	You notice some cut marks on your friend's arm. How do you feel and what would you do?
Group Solution	
4.	Your friend says that there are arguments and shouting at home all the time and she is quite frightened. How do you feel and what would you do?
Group Solution	
5.	Your friend's pet dog has died and he is really upset in class. How do you feel and what would you do?
Group Solution	

Scenario Cards (Cont)

6.	Your friend says that she has thoughts of hurting herself. How do you feel and what would you do?
Group Solution	
7.	Your friend is avoiding eating at meal times, although he talks about food a lot. How do you feel and what would you do?
Group Solution	
8.	Your friend is worried about an exam and asks to sit next to you so that she can copy your work. How would feel and what would you do?
Group Solution	
9.	Your friend says that his mum is depressed and is not looking after the family anymore. There is no food in the house or any clean clothes. How would you feel and what would you do?
Group Solution	
10.	Your friend doesn't want to come out to play anymore and just stays in her room. How do you feel and what would you do?
Group Solution	

Theme Two: What Helps and What Does Not?

Lesson 2: Mental Health Services for Young People

Introduction

This session encourages pupils to consider why people do not access the support and help they need. It also provides an opportunity to be creative and design a specific service for young people. The teacher facilitates a discussion around what pupils think they would need if they had to access support. This builds on the scenario activity.

Resources

- Sometimes My Brain Hurts folders.
- Access to the internet.
- Mental Health Services for Young People activity page.
- Pens and paper.

Aims

- To encourage pupils to consider what they would wish for, in a service specifically for them.
- To review why people do not seek help and support when they first realise that they need it.

Method

Starting the Session

Some pupils may have prior knowledge of services if they have attended themselves or with a family member or friend so the importance of the ground rules is particularly relevant for this session.

Activity

Mental Health Services for Young People

Pupils are given the opportunity to design a service specifically for young people. This works well as a group activity providing all individuals have the opportunity to share their ideas. The teacher may wish to select groups or allow pupils to choose for themselves. There is no limit to funding available, this enables them to be really imaginative. The teacher highlights how services may vary and there should be a number of options. Some suggestions might include art therapy, meditation and alternative therapies. The pupils do not only have to include medical interventions, they might like to create a garden for relaxation or a music room. They may use the internet for additional ideas.

Activity pages are provided for pupils to promote what their service has to offer. This could take the form of a poster advertising facilities, contact details, times of appointment and other information that the pupils wish to convey.

Discussion

Following their research and having created their services, the teacher facilitates discussion and feedback. It will be interesting to note common themes that emerge.

If posters are created, then the pupils could vote for which service they prefer and explain why. Perhaps if something is eye catching and colourful it would make the service more accessible and user-friendly for children and young people.

Mental Health Services for Young People

Design a service specifically for young people.

Theme Three: Why is Mental Health Important?

Lesson 1: Mental Health Quiz

Introduction

The session will clarify prior knowledge with a quiz that will confirm much of what the pupils have learned. It will also promote further discussion to highlight why we all need to have more information about mental health in the way we do for physical health.

Resources

- Sometimes My Brain Hurts folders.
- Mental Health Quiz activity page and answers.

Aim

- For pupils to revisit prior knowledge and clarify some points of understanding.

Method

Starting the Session

As with all previous sessions the ground rules are highlighted to ensure safety.

Activity

Mental Health Quiz

The teacher makes copies of the quiz for all pupils and hands them out for them to complete. The idea at this stage is for pupils to complete them on their own although it is not designed as a test.

Discussion

Following completion of the quiz, the teacher will ask pupils for feedback before giving the correct answers. Some of the questions are ambiguous, this is deliberate and again highlights the complex nature of mental health conditions.

Mental Health Quiz

Name:

Complete the following quiz.

Questions	True	False
1. I in 4 young people will experience a mental health problem at some stage in their lives.		
2. Mental health problems affect lazy people.		
3. Once you have a mental health problem you never recover.		
4. Girls have more eating disorders than boys.		
5. Depression lasts for years.		
6. Medication doesn't work.		
7. People stop self-harming when they get older.		
8. Everyone knows when a person is mentally unwell.		
9. Many more people have mental health problems than diabetes.		
10. Exercise and activity will improve mental health.		

Mental Health Quiz Answers

Questions	Answers
1. 1 in 4 young people will experience a mental health problem at some stage in their lives.	True. Mental health problems are much more common than people realise and also many conditions go undiagnosed, so this figure is probably an underestimate.
2. Mental health problems affect lazy people.	False. There is widespread misunderstanding that mental health problems are in some way a choice and that if people are lazy they use depression as an excuse.
3. Once you have a mental health problem you never recover.	False. The vast majority of people with mental health problems will recover, there are some who may become unwell again and some who also have ongoing problems.
4. Girls have more eating disorders than boys.	True, although this might be because girls are more willing to admit to having a problem.
5. Depression lasts for years.	True and False. The condition is very variable and will alter for each individual so while some people may have a problem for a long time, others will recover very quickly.
6. Medication doesn't work.	True and False. Mental health problems are much more complex than physical ones and while specific medication works for some individuals it does not necessarily work for all and adjustment and trial of certain medication might have to be explored. Not everyone with a mental health problem will need medication as there are alternative therapies such as counselling.
7. People stop self-harming when they get older.	False. Self-harming behaviour does not just affect young people there are much older people who continue to use it as a coping strategy.

Mental Health Quiz Answers (Cont)

Questions	Answers
8. Everyone knows when a person is mentally unwell.	False. Many people who have a mental health problem become very good at hiding it and as many other people do not know how to recognise mental distress they completely miss the signs.
9. Many more people have mental health problems than diabetes.	True. Because diabetes does not carry the stigma associated with mental health problems it gets talked about, therefore most people believe it is more common than psychosis for example.
10. Exercise and activity will improve mental health.	True. There is much evidence to suggest that exercise promotes positive mental health in the way it improves physical health. Some GP surgeries actually prescribe exercise for people with mental health problems. When we exercise, the body produces endorphins which help to lift mood, so it naturally follows that mental health will be improved.

Theme Three: Why is Mental Health Important?

Lesson 2: A-Z of Mental Health

Introduction

This session is designed to extend the knowledge of the pupils and encourage them to write a positive account of all they have learned so far. It also highlights again the use of language.

Resources

- Sometimes My Brain Hurts folders.
- Glossary of Terms. (Part Four).
- Pens and paper.
- A-Z of Mental Health activity page.
- Pupil Evaluation sheets.

Aims

- For pupils to reflect upon their developing knowledge and put the newly acquired language into perspective.
- To identify gaps in knowledge and understanding.

Method

Starting the Session

Ground rules are revisited.

Activity

A-Z of Mental Health

Pupils are asked to take the A-Z activity pages and write a short sentence or piece for each of the words to demonstrate their knowledge and understanding. This might be a definition or a descriptive statement. The teacher may need to refer to the glossary of terms to ensure that the pupils are recording correct information for their folders. There is an example for each that can be shared with the pupils, however, they should be encouraged to think of their own examples. The statements or descriptions are to be written in a positive light, which will emphasise the importance of stigma and discrimination awareness.

Discussion

When pupils have completed their A-Z sheets they are asked for feedback and comparisons are made between the statements and sentences created. This provides another opportunity for questions and answers to clear up any misunderstandings. The evaluation sheets are given out at the end of the lesson.

A-Z of Mental Health

A	Anxiety
B	Bipolar Disorder
C	Continuum
D	Depression
E	Eating Disorders
F	Fear
G	Getting Help
H	Hallucinations
I	Information
J	Judgement
K	Knowledge
L	Limitations
M	Medication

A-Z of Mental Health (Cont)

N	Normal
O	Obsessive Compulsive Disorder
P	Psychosis
Q	Questions
R	Reactions
S	Stigma
T	Treatment
U	Understanding
V	Voices in Your Head
W	Wellness Recovery Action Plan
X	Excluded
Y	Young People
Z	Schizophrenia

Year 5 Pupil Evaluation

1.	Did the lessons in the programme help you to understand a little bit more about mental health? Yes No
2.	Which session did you prefer most? Please explain why.
3.	Please tick all the subjects you have learned about: • Risk, resilience and mood states. • Myth or reality. • Problem scenarios. • Services for young people. • Mental health quiz. • A-Z of mental health.
4.	Please write three things you learned from the programme: 1. 2. 3.
5.	Is there anything else that you would like to learn that was not covered in this programme?

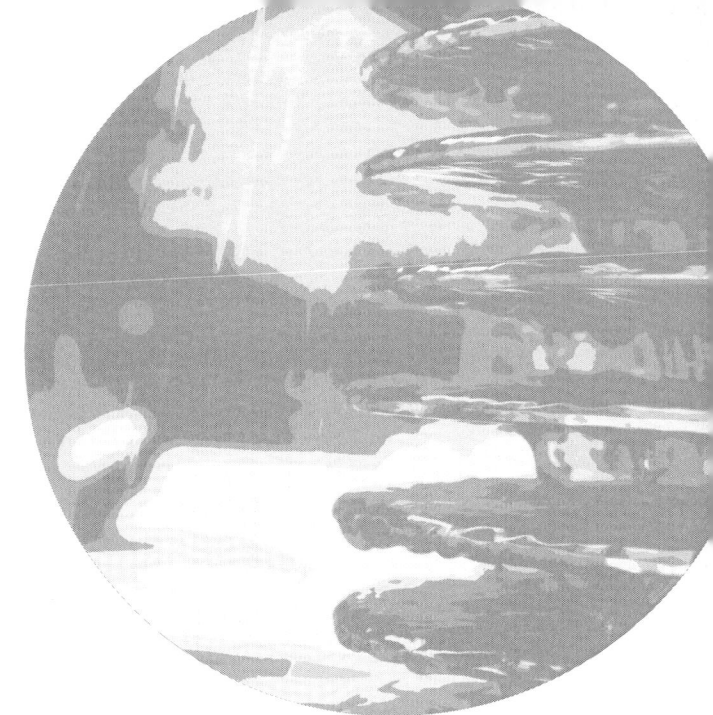

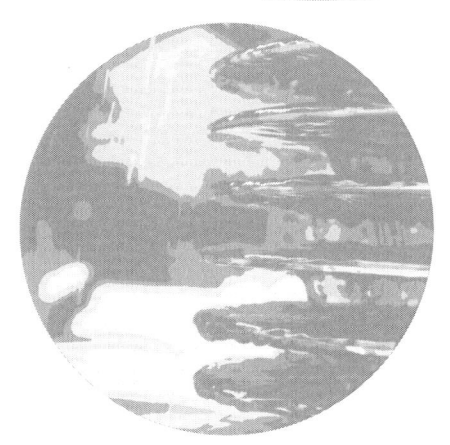

Year 6

Summary

Summary

The aim of the sessions for Year 6 pupils is not only, as with previous years, to build upon their existing knowledge and understanding, but also to encourage them to ask questions, challenge stigma and develop better coping strategies for their own mental and emotional wellbeing.

> Children who are troubled cannot flourish.

> (Place2b, 2011)

Pupils are encouraged to explore the subject of mental ill health in much more detail themselves in the first session and then present their findings to the rest of the class. The aim of this is to extend their knowledge and understanding of specific conditions.

Pupils are asked to consider the language around mental health and also to develop their listening skills further by practising talking about concerns. They are encouraged to reflect upon times when they have felt truly listened to and been given high positive regard, and also times when they have not and how that felt.

The impact of mental health problems can be enormous for some individuals who have lost their jobs, their homes and have damaged relationships beyond repair. There is an exercise that emphasises this aspect of poor mental health for pupils to consider.

The final session introduces positive psychology, sometimes referred to as the 'happiness' programme. Mental Health First Aid England always has a session on this during their training courses, as the subject of mental health can be very challenging and stir up strong emotions for people. The key message here is that having highlighted how important family and friends are in providing support for people who are experiencing mental distress, in order to provide support they need to be in a good place themselves. This means that their own levels of resilience and feeling able to cope have to be strong. When you are supporting someone who is distressed it is vitally important that you take care of your own emotional wellbeing. The session highlights how we all possess strengths and even when a day does not seem to be going well there are always some positive aspects to it and you just need to train your mind to find them.

In order to be really well prepared to deliver the sessions for Year 6, the teacher needs to start collecting magazines and newspapers that have articles or make reference to mental health. While the pupils will be researching mental health and mental illness on the internet, they will also be required to explore how mental health is portrayed through other forms of media.

Ground Rules Example

1. Be polite to all people.

2. Respect others' opinions.

3. Put your hand up if you want to speak.

4. Only one person speaks at a time.

5. You have the right to pass.

6. Listen to who is speaking.

7. Talk about yourself and let other people talk for themselves.

8. Be thoughtful and considerate at all times.

Many Year 6 pupils will not have heard the word 'confidentiality' or understand what it means, therefore it is a good idea to introduce it as part of the ground rules. This is quite difficult as the definition refers to speaking or writing in confidence, between us, classified, hush hush, private, off the record and secret, whereas many of the messages within the programme encourage children to talk about worries and concerns. It is important for the teacher to explain that talking about other people is not permitted within the lessons, and many of the suggested ground rules incorporate the essence of confidentiality.

Additional rules may be added or existing ones adapted to ensure that the group achieves ownership of the ground rules.

It is advisable to revisit the ground rules at the start of every lesson to enable pupils to feel safe and therefore able to contribute to discussions and activities and gain more from the sessions.

Theme One: What is Mental Health and Mental Illness?

Lesson 1: Facts and Figures

Introduction

While for previous year groups much of the information has been presented to the pupils, these first two sessions for Year 6 pupils encourages them to research mental health information and statistics for themselves and develop their knowledge.

Resources

- Sometimes My Brain Hurts folders.
- Facts and Figures activity pages.
- Mental Health Conditions handout.
- Access to the internet.

Aims

- To research mental health.
- To explore facts and figures associated with mental health.
- To present findings to the rest of the class and extend knowledge further.

Method

Starting the Session

Pupils are reminded of the importance of ground rules and the teacher starts the lesson by highlighting how a sensitive approach should be adopted at all times during these sessions. As with previous lessons, it is very important that everyone feels safe and able to contribute to the session. Pupils are asked to remember that mental health problems affect many people, this is not their choice, and respect should be shown towards people in the classroom who may have experienced problems themselves or with members of their family and friends. There are some suggested ground rules at the start of this section but the teacher is advised to ask for additional rules or amend existing ones to suit the needs of the group and ensure that they have ownership of them.

Activity

Mental Health Conditions

Pupils are divided into groups of three to work on this particular activity. They are given a mental health condition from the list to research. The list provides some appropriate websites for pupils to explore in order to find out more about each topic area. They are asked to consider the following:

- What is the mental health condition?
- How many people does it affect? As some conditions affect certain age groups and there is a gender bias, pupils are also asked to consider this.
- Signs and symptoms.
- Probable outcomes.
- Treatment.

Facts and Figures

The teacher also gives out the Facts and Figures activity page and the pupils start exploring their allocated subject area. When they have answered the questions posed on the activity page, they are then asked to present their findings to the rest of the class.

Discussion

The teacher will facilitate discussion following each presentation done in the previous activity and ask how much the pupils already knew. Were there any particularly shocking discoveries during their research and has the activity changed their thinking regarding mental health conditions?

Mental Health Conditions

1. Depression.

2. Anxiety.

3. Phobias.

4. Bipolar disorder.

5. Schizophrenia.

6. Eating disorders.

7. Self-harm.

8. Obsessive compulsive disorder.

9. Post traumatic stress disorder.

10. Psychosis.

Websites

www.youngminds.org.uk
www.time-to-change.org.uk
www.mentalhealthfoundation.org.uk
www.mhfayouth.org.uk
www.theplace2be.org.uk/why_it_matters.aspx?menuid=2
www.nice.org
www.samaritans.org.uk
www.rethink.org
www.shift.org.uk
www.papyrus-uk.org

Facts and Figures about Mental Health

Name of condition:

How many people does it affect?

Signs and symptoms:

Probable outcomes:

Treatment:

Additional information:

Theme One: What is Mental Health and Mental Illness?

Lesson 2: Mental Health and The Media

Introduction

Following on from the previous session, pupils are encouraged to explore how mental health is portrayed in the media. They may do this by considering all forms of media including newspapers and magazines, the internet, films and television. The teacher starts the session by asking where pupils get information on mental health from and also if the pupils think it is accurate.

Resources

- Sometimes My Brain Hurts folders.
- Access to the internet.
- Mental Health and The Media activity page.
- Magazines and newspapers.

Aims

- To explore how mental health is portrayed in the media.
- To consider the role of organisations in supporting positive mental health.

Method

Starting the Session

Ground rules are to be revisited and pupils reminded to adopt a sensitive approach to the session. The teacher provides some magazines and newspapers for the pupils to explore. If this is not possible then the pupils can access them via the internet.

Activity

Mental Health and The Media

Pupils are divided into groups of three for this activity and encouraged to find out as much as they can regarding media coverage on mental health. The groups do not have to be the same ones used in the previous lesson, the teacher might find it is useful to mix groups up to gain more varied feedback. Using the activity page, the pupils have to answer various questions including:

- Is the information accurate?
- Is the story told in a positive light?
- Is there evidence of stigma and discrimination?

- How high is the profile of the story? For example, is it buried under many other potentially more interesting stories?

Discussion

When the pupils have completed the activity page they are asked to provide feedback to the rest of the class regarding their findings and opinions. The teacher uses this opportunity to facilitate a lively and interactive discussion that will aim to explore the way in which mental health is reported in the media. It is also important to highlight the stigma and discrimination that may be apparent in the articles or stories.

If time allows the pupils are asked how a more positive angle could be achieved with the stories they have found. They could re-write them using the most appropriate and correct language that they have learned in previous sessions. Also they could consider how positive messages about organisations that promote positive mental health as well as providing help and support could be publicised.

Pupils who have watched TV soaps could give examples of how some mental health conditions have been portrayed and discuss if they think the storyline has handled the subject matter effectively and sensitively. The teacher can emphasise that at the end of some programmes dealing with subjects such as mental illness, an announcement is given to signpost viewers to organisations that can provide help and support if the programme has raised issues that cause distress. The same cannot be said for the newspapers or websites.

Mental Health and The Media

Source of information:

Summary of story or article:

How accurate is this information?

How did you find out about the accuracy?

What is your opinion regarding whether this seemed positive or negative?

Any evidence of stigma, discrimination or negative language?

How high profile was the story?

Theme Two: What Helps and What Does Not?

Lesson 1: Our Needs

Introduction

The aim of this session is to challenge some of the messages pupils receive about what they need in order to be content and well, mentally. There is evidence to suggest that our society has become very materialistic and that in order to thrive we need all sorts of goods. However, research by the New Economics Foundation (2008) reveals quite the opposite and challenges this viewpoint. It goes further to propose five ways to wellbeing. Following the activity pupils will be encouraged to consider them and how they achieve them each day.

Resources

- Sometimes My Brain Hurts folders.
- Our Needs activity page.
- Pens and paper.
- Five Ways to Wellbeing handout.
- My Five Ways to Wellbeing activity page.

Aims

- To encourage pupils to consider what we need to stay mentally and emotionally well.
- To challenge some of the stereotypical views from the media that we need materialistic goods.
- To think about applying the five ways to wellbeing.

Method

The teacher should prepare enough statements for each group of pupils to explore.

Starting the Session

Ground rules should be emphasised as with all previous sessions.

Activity

Our Needs

Pupils are given the 12 statements and asked to discuss them in their groups. The aim is for the groups to agree on which of the statements are true and which are false. They then continue with the activity and arrange the statements in order of importance, for example, is needing to feel safe more important that being loved?

Five Ways to Wellbeing

The teacher issues the Five Ways to Wellbeing handout and asks pupils to consider how they meet the criteria. Specifically, how do they connect with people, how are they active, how do they take notice, keep learning and give? The teacher is also advised to share how they meet the criteria as this will provide the pupils with examples. This emphasises what is important and clarifies the message from the Our Needs activity. The pupils then complete the activity page, My Five Ways to Wellbeing identifying what they already do or plan to do.

Discussion

The pupils are asked to share their ways to wellbeing and determine if there are common themes that emerge. The teacher will facilitate a discussion that highlights that there are no absolutely correct or wrong answers as people find differing ways to connect or give and fulfil the five ways to wellbeing.

The completed activity pages are then added to the pupils' folders so they may refer back to them.

Our Needs

Everyone needs love.

We need expensive designer clothes.

Everyone needs someone to talk to and someone to listen.

We need to be really talented at something.

We need cuddles and close connections with people.

We need to feel safe.

Our Needs (Cont)

We need to be very popular.

We need lots of money.

We need healthy food for our mental as well as physical health.

We all need physical activity to stay mentally well.

We all need friends.

Smiling is good for you, laughter is better, cheering is best!

Five Ways to Wellbeing

1. Connect

Connect with people around you, with family, friends and neighbours, at home, school and in your community. Think of these as the cornerstones of your life and invest time in developing them. Building these connections will support and enrich you every day.

2. Be Active

Go for a walk or run, step outside, cycle, play a game, dance. Exercising makes you feel good. Most importantly, discover a physical activity that you enjoy and that suits your level of fitness.

3. Take Notice

Be curious, catch sight of beautiful things and remark on the unusual. Notice the changing seasons, savour the moment, whether you are walking to school, eating lunch or talking to friends. Be aware of the world around you and what you are feeling. Reflecting on your experiences will help you to appreciate what matters to you.

4. Keep Learning

Try something new, rediscover an old interest. Sign up for a course, take on a different responsibility at school. Learn to play an instrument or how to cook your favourite food. Set a challenge that you will enjoy achieving. Learning new things will make you more confident as well as being fun.

5. Give

Do something nice for a friend, thank someone, smile, volunteer your time or join a group. Look out as well as in, seeing yourself and your happiness linked to a wider community can be incredibly rewarding and creates connections with people around you.

My Five Ways to Wellbeing

1. Connect. I connect with people:

2. Be Active. I am active:

3. Take Notice. I take notice:

4. Keep Learning. I keep learning:

5. Give. I give:

Theme Two: What Helps and What Does Not?

Lesson 2: Coping Strategies for Reducing Stress and Increasing Resilience

Introduction

As with many of the previous sessions there are no absolute right or wrong answers and people are entitled to their opinion and this should be respected. Particularly when it comes to coping strategies, what might be very helpful for one person might increase levels of anxiety in another, and the aim is for the pupils to discuss and consider all the options. Pupils are asked to focus specifically upon what they do to cope when feeling stressed. They are asked to consider ways in which they could increase their resilience in order to cope when things are not going well for them. This will provide them with a resource of their own to refer back to when they are feeling unable to cope with a situation. This in turn enhances their skills and capacity to take care of their own mental and emotional wellbeing.

Resources

- Sometimes My Brain Hurts folders.
- Pens and paper.
- Coping Strategies activity page.
- Good Listening activity page.
- Listening and Helpful Talking activity page.

Aims

- To encourage pupils to consider how they cope when under stress.
- To develop listening skills further.
- For pupils to think about who they turn to when they are worried or need to talk.

Method

Starting the Session

The session should start with the ground rules. It is a good idea to check out pupils understanding of stress and resilience, what do these words mean to them? The teacher can highlight for pupils that not all stress is bad and emphasise the example of taking exams or performing, when you need adrenaline in order to feel able to perform at your highest level. If you were completely relaxed you could easily forget things and not achieve your best results. A useful way of describing resilience is 'bouncebackability', essentially being able to bounce back and cope when life delivers a setback for you.

The teacher should prepare the Coping Strategies activity pages so that every pupil has a copy of their own for their folder. The teacher then needs to make the Good Listening statements into cards by printing them and cutting them up so that groups of pupils can arrange them in order of preference.

Activity

Coping Strategies

The teacher should issue the Coping Strategy activity statements and ask the pupils to rate them in order of importance. When the activity is completed the teacher facilitates a discussion on the feedback and establishes areas of agreement or not.

There will be some common themes, although it is important to realise that what is helpful for one individual, might not be the choice of another. When people make a decision and identify that they need to take action and they decide what route they will take this is very empowering and far more meaningful than when a person feels that they are being 'done to'. The 'I think I know what is best for you' approach does not apply in this particular set of circumstances.

Listening

Pupils are asked to work in small groups and discuss the listening statements. They are then asked to rank them in order of importance. When each group has completed the activity they are asked to provide feedback and share their views on what good listening means to them.

Discussion

Finally, the teacher issues the Listening and Helpful Talking activity page. The aim of this final activity page is for pupils to learn about the importance of good listening. Mental Health First Aid England regard non-judgemental listening as a key aspect of providing support for people who are experiencing mental health problems, and also highlights how feeling heard is good for everyone's resilience and self-esteem.

Pupils are asked to reflect and complete the sentences. They are then encouraged to think about whom they talk to when they are worried or feel anxious. When do they talk to them and what subjects might they share? It would be helpful for the teacher to provide some examples, such as struggling with school work, feeling left out of a group or people arguing at home. The teacher will facilitate feedback and again some common themes may emerge. When the activity pages are completed, they are added to the folders for future reference by the pupils.

Coping Strategies for Reducing Stress and Increasing Resilience

Rank in order of importance with 1 being the most important and 20 being the least important.

Strategy	Number
Seeing a film.	
Listening to music.	
Reading a book.	
Bottling up my worries.	
Playing on the computer.	
Getting angry.	
Staying in my room.	
Caring for pets.	
A good night's sleep.	
Family support.	
Being kind.	
Being connected.	
Noticing when something good happens even if it is small.	
Learning new things.	
Exercise.	
Helping someone else.	
Talking to friends.	
Seeing a doctor or nurse.	
Medication.	
Make my own decisions about what I share with my family/carers.	

Good Listening

You stop what you are doing and look at me.

You repeat what I have said to check your understanding.

You don't interrupt me while I am speaking.

You don't try to solve my problems or tell me not to worry.

You sit quietly with me.

You ask me how you can help.

You nod and make 'mmm' sounds to show you are listening.

You encourage me to continue talking by smiling at me.

You ask questions to help me to continue speaking.

Listening and Helpful Talking

Listening

A time I felt I was really listened to was:

A time when I felt I was not listened to was:

Helpful Talking

Who would you talk to first?

Next?

After that?

Last?

What else can you do?

Theme Three: Why is Mental Health Important?

Lesson 1: The Cost of Mental Ill Health

Introduction

Throughout the sessions for Year 6 pupils there has been a theme of challenging stigma and discrimination associated with mental ill health. This session builds upon that knowledge and understanding, and encourages pupils to consider what happens to a person when they become mentally unwell. It specifically focuses upon the impact and effect of mental illness and the losses that a person and their family might experience.

Resources

- Sometimes My Brain Hurts folders.
- Pens and papers.
- What does Mental Ill Health Cost? activity pages.

Aim

- For pupils to appreciate the impact of mental ill health and the consequences.

Method

Starting the Session

Ground rules should be emphasised as with all previous sessions. The teacher prepares the activity pages for the pupils to complete and also has the teacher notes of the possible answers to facilitate discussion at the end of the session. There is a space for pupils to write their own suggestions of impact and effect associated with mental illness.

Activity

What Does Mental Ill Health Cost?

This activity encourages pupils to consider the things that can be lost when a person becomes mentally unwell. The key message here is that people with mental health problems stand to lose much, not just in financial terms through loss of earnings but also their sense of self-worth and ability to maintain relationships.

This is quite a challenging activity for pupils to think about and they may need some additional guidance to gain the greatest understanding of the impact and effect of mental illness.

As with previous sessions, the teacher needs to be aware that some of the pupils might have first hand knowledge of the impact and therefore this session could prove upsetting for them. They should be encouraged to talk to the teacher after the session if they are worried and all pupils should be reminded of the ground rules if a pupil decides to share their experiences.

Discussion

The teacher facilitates the feedback and discussion to explore the pupils' findings and ideas around what a person with mental health problems might lose along with the impact and effect. The teacher can explain that some mental health problems are short-term and some last much longer. Again, this is an individual aspect as people's recovery time will vary depending upon the support they have available to them. This does not just mean therapeutic interventions or medication but most essentially support and care from family and friends and people who are important to the individual.

Teacher Notes: What does Mental Ill Health Cost?

Aspect	Impact and Effect
Loss of job through time off sick and being unreliable.	Many people with mental illness, such as depression or anxiety or both, really struggle when there is extra pressure at work and therefore take time off sick. It should also be pointed out to pupils that with adequate support many people could maintain their position and prove very reliable within the workplace. A key point here is that if there was less stigma and discrimination perhaps people would feel able to disclose when they felt that they were not coping so well and support could be put in place sooner to enable them to cope. They might not lose their job but have some suitable adjustments to enable them to fulfil their responsibilities.
Relationships that couldn't take the strain.	Sometimes it is very hard to understand what is going on for a person with a mental illness as their perspective might not appear very realistic. For people who experience panic attacks their fear is very real for them and the strain of supporting a person who does not seem to have the same reality as you may take its toll. Again, as with the previous point, with the right care and support relationships can be maintained and flourish. It is important for the person who is providing support for the individual who is unwell to have support for themselves.
Loss of home through inability to pay bills, rent/mortgage.	Clearly, if a person is unable to hold down a job their income will suffer and they may not be able to maintain their lifestyle.
Friends who got bored of trying to help!	It can be very demanding when a person is very depressed and can't see anything positive. Sometimes friends get very tired of trying to make a situation better for the person they care about, and if they feel they are not helping and it impacts in a negative way for them, they might stop calling. Pupils could discuss a situation when they found a friend difficult or very demanding of their time.

Teacher Notes: What does Mental Ill Health Cost? (Cont)

Aspect	Impact and Effect
May develop a dependence on drugs and alcohol.	When some people are mentally unwell they resort to taking drugs or alcohol to manage the negative feelings they are having. Some substances provide a numbing effect that enables the person to feel that they are able to cope. They may take something that helps them to relax or sleep so that they have a break from their painful thoughts and feelings. While drugs and alcohol might provide a brief respite from their pain, many individuals find they feel worse when the effect wears off.
Sense of self-worth.	Mental illnesses can distort a person's view of themselves. Some people who hear voices can become damaged by insults or derogatory comments. When a person is mentally unwell they sometimes lack the drive and energy to complete quite simple tasks and therefore feel a failure when they do not fulfil their own expectations.
Pride.	Sometimes people with mental illness lose their sense of pride, it can be easier to believe that you will fail.
Appearance.	When mental illness affects a person they can develop different priorities and mostly taking care of their appearance does not become one of them. It might be an early sign of an emerging mental illness when a person who has always taken great care of their appearance suddenly starts not bothering.
Lack of self-care through not washing, eating properly.	With moderate to severe depression and during the low phases with bipolar disorder a person might not complete even the most basic self-care. Most of us feel better when we have a shower, wash our hair and eat a good meal but mental illness can take this away. Again Mental Health First Aid highlights the importance of self-care.

Teacher Notes: What does Mental Ill Health Cost? (Cont)

Aspect	Impact and Effect
Ability to cope and maintaining resilience.	Mental illness can make people feel vulnerable and when life becomes difficult for them they are not able to cope in the way a very healthy person would be able to. For most individuals when life throws several things at them at once their resilience or ability to cope is extremely compromised and challenged. Pupils need to understand how resilience and vulnerability vary during a lifetime and even sometimes from day to day.
Appreciation, feeling nothing matters anymore.	Depression can remove a person's ability to enjoy things that they previously gained pleasure from. When a person feels very low they fail to see meaning in many things, even family and friends. During a psychotic episode a person could lose a great deal of time just sitting and not actually doing anything because they don't see the point. The encouraging aspect to consider here is that for some individuals it might be a very small trigger that brings enjoyment back to their lives. Again, this will vary from person to person.
Confidence, feeling I can't do it, I might fail.	This point links in with many others and reflects the lack of coping skills and resilience. When a person feels well and strong they are more likely to try something new, but all of us can appreciate the fear of failure, letting others down and feeling embarrassed. Pupils could be asked to consider their own fears and share if they wish.
Sense of humour, nothing makes me laugh anymore.	Mental illness is not funny, as with lack of enjoyment, people who have problems fail to see the funny side of things. Something that they might have found really funny when well, will not appear even faintly amusing when they are unwell.

Teacher Notes: What does Mental Ill Health Cost? (Cont)

Aspect	Impact and Effect
Possessions that were sold to support drugs/alcohol habit.	In order to buy substances and alcohol, especially if a person has lost their job, they might sell possessions or steal.
If I block out feelings, I feel better.	Ironically, while people with mental health problems need to talk to someone who will offer them support and understanding, when they are unwell they are much less likely to ask for support. Pupils could reflect upon who they talk to when worried and what might stop them, it could be that they feel judged.
Pupils own suggestions.	This box is deliberately left blank for pupils to write their own ideas down.

What does Mental Ill Health Cost?

Aspect	Impact and Effect
Loss of job through time off sick and being unreliable.	
Relationships that couldn't take the strain.	
Loss of home through inability to pay bills, rent/mortgage.	
Friends who got bored of trying to help!	
May develop a dependence on drugs or alcohol.	
Sense of self-worth.	
Pride.	
Appearance.	

What does Mental Ill Health Cost?

Aspect	Impact and Effect
Lack of self-care through not washing, eating properly.	
Ability to cope and maintaining resilience.	
Appreciation, feeling nothing matters anymore.	
Confidence, feeling I can't do it, I might fail.	
Sense of humour, nothing makes me laugh anymore.	
Possessions that were sold to support drugs/alcohol habit.	
If I block out feelings, I feel better.	
(Pupils own suggestions.)	

Theme Three: Why is Mental Health Important?

Lesson 2: Identifying Strengths – An Introduction to Positive Psychology

Introduction

Pupils have been encouraged to find out as much as they can about mental health conditions, including some facts and figures. Much of the information relating to mental ill health makes for fairly depressing reading, so the aim of this final session is to enable pupils to feel that they can cope. They have learned about how listening is very supportive and also how to ask for help themselves when they need it. Hopefully, they will have received some positive messages about recovery from mental health conditions and that there is no need to be frightened. They will have challenged stigma and discrimination and feel that they have much greater knowledge and understanding of quite a complex subject.

Resources

- Sometimes My Brain Hurts folders.
- Pens and paper.
- Identifying Strengths activity page.
- Positive Affirmations activity page.
- Plain sheets of A4 and tape.
- Evaluation sheets.

Aims

- To empower pupils to identify their strengths and coping skills further.
- To encourage pupils to focus upon positive elements in their lives.
- To learn how to give positive affirmations.

Method

Starting the Session

The teacher should print copies of the Identifying Strengths activity page for the pupils. They will also need a Positive Affirmations activity page each. The ground rules are revisited and emphasised as with previous sessions.

Activity

Identifying Strengths

The pupils are encouraged to work in groups to identify their strengths. While some pupils will find this activity relatively easy, others may find it quite difficult and require help with it. As with previous sessions, the teacher could provide some examples of their own strengths or those of others they admire, this will give permission for the pupils to engage without feeling that they are boasting. Pupils could be asked to consider people they admire or who have strengths they would wish to develop. They are reminded that the strengths do not always have to relate to big things as very often a small gesture or a comment from a caring individual can make a huge difference to all of us, not only those with mental health problems. Many pupils will have a strong sense of right and wrong so the 'fair' strength could be a particular one that they can identify with.

The aim of the session is to highlight that everybody has strengths and it might be that we are not aware of them even though others find them obvious. Pupils are encouraged to make a note of their strengths in their folders. In order to be more focused, pupils are asked to identify their top five strengths from the list provided.

Positive Affirmations

The Positive Affirmations activity pages are handed out and pupils are asked to work in pairs to complete the first two sentences. They complete the rest of the form themselves and then the teacher can facilitate feedback and discussion before handing out the evaluation sheets.

An additional activity that captures feedback from the whole class is for pupils to have a plain sheet of paper taped to their backs. Everyone mingles around and each pupil writes positive comments about their fellow pupil on the sheets. The teacher can then read out the comments and the completed sheet of positive affirmations can be included in the folder. This makes a really nice reference point when pupils are feeling that they are not coping so well, they could visit their sheets and rediscover their strengths, which in turn will boost their self-esteem and ability to cope as well as improving resilience.

Discussion

The final discussion is an open question and answer session to clear up any misunderstandings and clarify any outstanding points that have arisen during the programme. If time allows pupils could design illustrations to accompany the strength cards and add them to their folders.

Finally pupils are asked to complete the evaluation forms.

Identifying Strengths

What are your top five strengths?

Adventurous	Assertive
Attentive	Brave
Capable	Careful
Caring	Cooperative
Committed	Confident
Contented	Creative
Curious	Determined
Different	Encouraging
Enthusiastic	Energetic
Fair	Flexible
Forgiving	Friendly
Generous	Gentle
Happy	Hardworking
Helpful	Honest
Hopeful	Humble
Humorous	Independent
Kind	Loving
Loyal	Open
Organised	Patient
Peaceful	Playful
Practical	Protective
Purposeful	Relaxed
Resourceful	Reliable
Resilient	Responsible
Respectful	Skilful
Strong	Thoughtful
Understanding	Wise

Positive Affirmations

Something I really like about you is:

A really individual thing about you is:

Three things that went well today are:

1.

2.

3.

I feel happy when:

Year 6 Pupil Evaluation

I.	Did the lessons in the programme help you to understand a little bit more about mental health? Yes No
2.	Which session did you prefer most? Please explain why.

3.	Please tick all the subjects you have learned about:
	
	    • Facts and figures.
	    • Mental health and the media.
	    • Our needs.
	    • Coping strategies to reduce stress and increase resilience.
	    • The cost of mental health.
	    • Identifying strengths, an introduction to positive psychology.

4.	Please write three things that you learned from the mental health programme. I. 2. 3.
5.	Is there anything else that you would like to learn that was not covered in this programme?

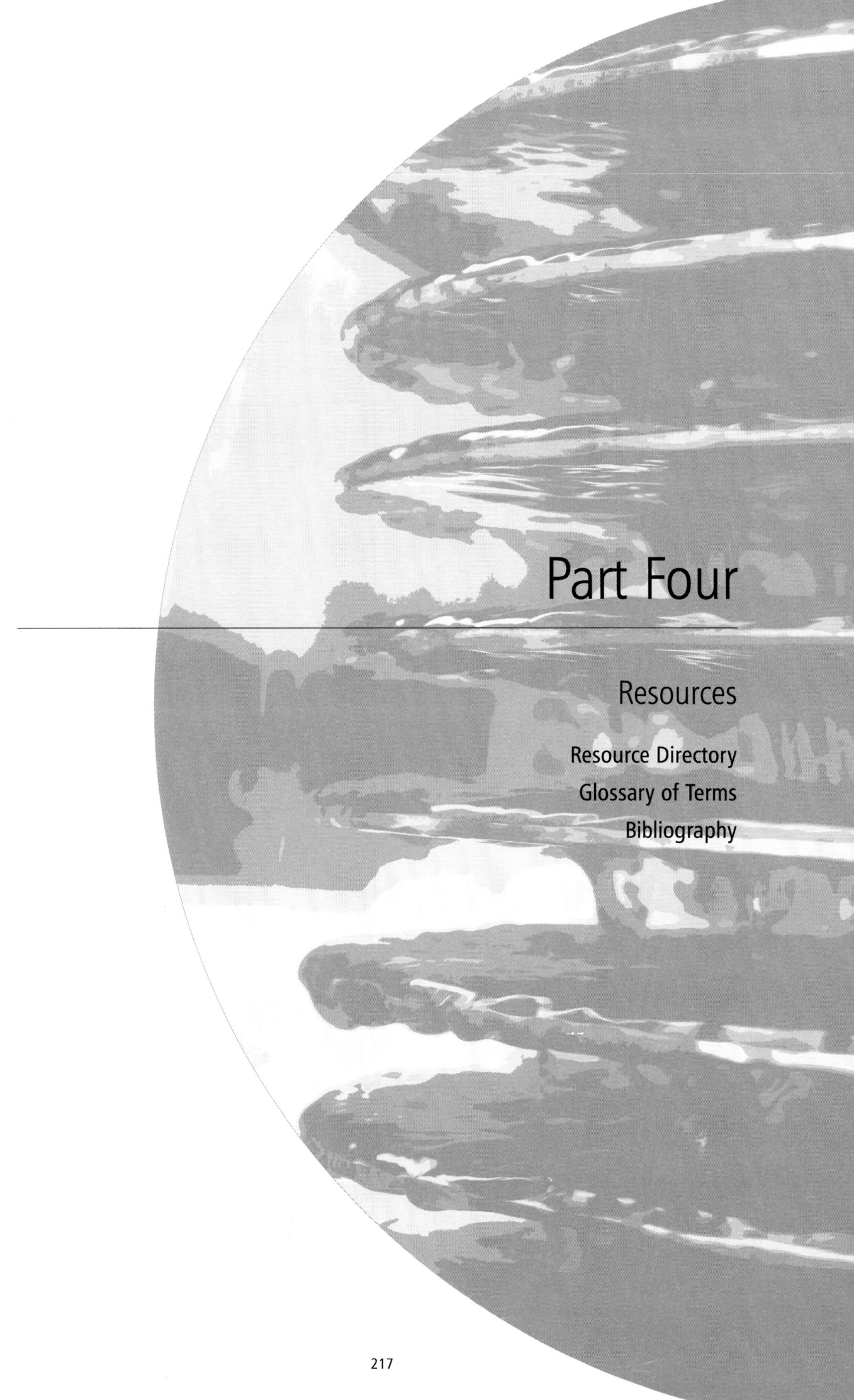

Part Four

Resources

Resource Directory
Glossary of Terms
Bibliography

Resource Directory

Websites

ChildLine
www.childline.org.uk

Department for Education
www.dfe.gov.uk

Mental Health First Aid England Youth
www.mhfaengland.org/youth-mhfa

Mindful Employer
www.mindfulemployer.net

National Institute for Health and Clinical Excellence
www.nice.org.uk

New Economics Foundations Five Ways to Wellbeing
www.neweconomics.org

No Health Without Mental Health
www.dh.gov.uk/mentalhealthstrategy

NSPCC
www.nspcc.org.uk

Papyrus
www.papyrus-uk.org

Rethink
www.rethink.org

Samaritans
www.samaritans.org.uk

Shift

www.shift.org.uk

The Children and Young People's Mental Health Coalition
www.cypmhc.org.uk/resources/improving_children_and_young_peoples_mental_health

The Mental Health Foundation

www.mentalhealthfoundation.org.uk

The Place2be

www.theplace2be.org.uk/why_it_matters.aspx?menuid=2

Time to Change

www.time-to-change.org.uk

Young Minds

www.youngminds.org.uk

Useful Reading

Becoming Emotionally Intelligent. C, Corrie. Network Educational Press, Stafford.

Celebrating Strengths. J, Fox Eades. CAPP Press, London.

Detoxing Childhood. S, Palmer. Orion Publishing, London.

Developing the Emotionally Literate School. K, Weare. Paul Chapman Publishing, London.

Emotional Health and Wellbeing. B, Heaven. Optimus Education, London.

Emotional Intelligence. D, Goleman. Bantam Books, New York.

Social and Emotional Aspects of Learning. HMSO, Department for Education and Skills.

Teaching Happiness. R, MacConville. Optimus Education, London.

The Little Book of Bereavement for Schools. I, Gilbert. Crown House Publishing, Carmarthan.

The School I'd Like. C, Burke and I, Grosvenor. Routledge Farmer, London.

The Young Mind. S, Bailey and M, Shooter. Bantam Press, Ealing.

Why are they so Weird?: What's Really Going on in a Teenager's Brain. B, Strauch. Bloomsbury Publishing PLC, London.

Glossary of Terms

Anxiety: A normal and a natural response useful in dangerous situations and experienced by everybody at some time. It can vary in severity.

Anxiety disorder: This is different from anxiety as it is more severe, long lasting and it interferes with life.

Bipolar disorder: A severe mental illness with a long course, usually characterised by episodes of depressed mood alternating with episodes of elated mood and increased activity (mania or hypomania). For many people, however, the predominant experience is of low mood. In its more severe forms, bipolar disorder is associated with significant impairment of personal and social functioning.

CAMHS: Child and Adolescent Mental Health Services.

Cognitive Behavioural Therapy (CBT): A type of therapy that aims to help people to manage their problems by changing how they think (cognitive) and act (behavioural), which can help them to feel better about life.

Depression: A loss of interest and enjoyment in ordinary things and experiences of low mood and a range of associated emotional, cognitive, physical and behavioural symptoms (www.nice.org.uk).

Eating disorder: This involves a disturbance of eating habits or weight control behaviour that results in impairment of physical health or which affects the person's psychological and social functioning.

Mental health: Good or positive mental health is more than the absence or management of mental health problems, it is the foundation for the wellbeing and effective functioning both for individuals and for their communities.

Mental health problem: A phrase used in the government strategy as an umbrella term to denote the full range of diagnosable mental illnesses and disorders, including personality disorder. Mental health problems may be more or less common and acute or longer lasting and may vary in severity. They may manifest themselves in different ways at different ages and may present as behavioural problems, for example, in children and young people. Some people object to the use of terms such as 'mental health problem' on the grounds that they medicalise ways of thinking and feeling and do not acknowledge the many factors that can prevent people from reaching their potential. While recognising these concerns and the stigma attached to mental ill health, however, there is no universally acceptable terminology that can be used.

National Institute of Clinical Excellence (NICE): An independent organisation that provides advice and guidance on cost and effectiveness of drugs and treatments.

Obsessive compulsive disorder (OCD): This is the least common form of anxiety disorder and is largely associated with fear of contamination and presents as repetitive behaviours.

Panic attacks: A sudden onset of intense fear that can develop rapidly and is inappropriate for the circumstances.

Phobias: These can cause people to restrict their activities and can be very specific. The fear experienced by the individual appears persistent, excessive and unreasonable and may prevent a person from living their life the way they would wish.

Psychosis: Psychosis affects a person's mind and causes changes to the way that they think, feel and behave. A person who experiences psychosis may be unable to distinguish between reality and their imagination. They may have hallucinations or delusions. Psychosis is an umbrella term to describe mental health conditions and a psychotic episode may be caused by schizophrenia or bipolar disorder.

Post traumatic stress disorder (PTSD): PTSD can develop after a distressing event, either where the person has been actively involved or has witnessed the harm of another as in the case of domestic abuse.

Recovery: This term has developed a specific meaning in mental health that is not the same as, although is related to, clinical recovery. It can be defined as a deeply personal, unique process of changing one's attitudes, values, feelings, goals, skills or roles. It is a way of living a satisfying, hopeful and contributing life, even with limitations caused by the illness. Recovery involves the development of new meaning and purpose in one's life.

Resilience: An important aspect of wellbeing and mental health, the ability to cope with **adverse** circumstances, either as an individual or in a community.

Schizophrenia: A major psychiatric disorder or cluster of disorders, characterised by psychotic symptoms that alter a person's perceptions and thoughts that affect their behaviour. Each person with the disorder will have a unique combination of symptoms and experiences.

Self-harm is a behaviour not an illness. People self-harm to cope with emotional distress or to communicate their pain.

Stress: The body's reaction to a change that requires a physical, mental or emotional adjustment or response. Stress can come from any situation or thought that makes you feel frustrated, angry, nervous or anxious. Stress is caused by an existing stress-causing factor or stressor. Dealing with a serious illness or caring for someone who is ill can cause a great deal of stress.

Suicide: The action of killing oneself, which might be intentional or accidental.

Wellbeing: Sometimes referred to as mental and emotional wellbeing, 'A positive state of mind and body, feeling safe and able to cope, with a sense of connection with people, communities and the wider environment,' (Department of Health, 2011).

Bibliography

Adelstein, A. & Mardon, C. (2010) Suicide rates in the UK 1991-2008. *Office of National Statistics.*

www.ons.gov.uk/ons/rel/subnational-health4/suicides-in-the-united-kingdom/2010/stb-statistical-bulletin.html

Aked, J., Marks, N., Cordon, C. & Thompson, S. (2008) *Five Ways to Wellbeing.* London: The New Economic Foundation.

www.neweconomics.org

Alexander, T. (2004) *A Bright Future for All. Scotland: The Mental Health Foundation.*

www.mentalhealth.org.uk/html/content/a_bright_future_for_all_intro.pdf

Bailey, S. & Shooter, M. (2009) *The Young Mind.* Ealing: Bantam Press.

Brander, N. (2003) 'Drinking Water in Schools'. *Nursing Times.* net, Vol. 99, Issue 01, p50.

Burke, C. & Grosvenor, I. (2003) *The School I'd Like.* London: Routledge Farmer.

Centre for Economic Performance's Mental Health Policy Group (2006) The Depression Report.

Chandiramani, R. (2011) 'Is ECM Defunct?' *Children and Young People Now.* London: Haymarket Professional Publications Ltd.

Child and Adolescent Component of the National Survey of Mental Health and Wellbeing (2000)
mbsonline.gov.au/Internet/main/publishing.nsf/Content/70DA14F816CC7A8FCA257288 00104564/$File/young.pdf

Corrie, C. (2003) *Becoming Emotionally Intelligent.* Stafford: Network Educational Press.

Department for Education (2003) Excellence and Enjoyment, a Strategy for Primary Schools. HMSO.

Department for Education (2012) Healthy Schools. HMSO.

Department for Education and Skills (2004) Social and Emotional Aspects of Learning. HMSO.

Department of Health (2004) *National Service Framework for Children, Young People and Maternity Services*. London: The Stationary Office.

Department of Health (2009) Healthy Lives: Brighter Futures.
www.dh.gov.uk/en/Publicationsandstatistics/Publications/
PublicationsPolicyAndGuidance/DH_094400

Department of Health (2010) Confident Communities, Brighter Futures. HMSO.

Department of Health (2011) No Health without Mental Health.
www.dh.gov.uk/mentalhealthstrategy

Fox, C. & Hawton, K. (2004) *Deliberate Self-Harm in Adolescence*. London: Jessica Kingsley Publishers.

Fox Eades, J. (2008) *Celebrating Strengths*. London: CAPP Press.

Goleman, D. (1995) *Emotional Intelligence*. New York: Bantam Books.

Green, H., McGinnity, A., Meltzer, H., Ford, T. & Goodman, R. (2005) *Mental Health of Children and Young People in Great Britain*. Office of National Statistics.

Hawton, K., Rodham, K. & Evans, E. (2002) 'Deliberate Self-Harm in Adolescents: Self Report Survey in Schools in England'. *British Medical Journal* 325 (7374), p1207-1211.

Hawton, K., Hall, S. & Simkin, S. (2003) 'Deliberate self-harm in adolescents: a study of characteristics and trends in Oxford 1990-2000'. *Journal of Child Psychology and Psychiatry* 44(8), p1191-1198.

Heaven, B. (2008) *Emotional Health and Wellbeing*. London: Optimus Education.

Home Office (2010) Equality Act.
www.homeoffice.gov.uk/equalities/equality-act/

HM Treasury (2005) *The Economic and Social Costs of Crime*. Home Office Research Study.

Jackson, C., Hill, K. & Lavis, P. (2008) *Child and Adolescent Mental Health Today*. Brighton: Pavillion.

Kim-Cohen, J., Caspi, A., Moffitt, T. E. et al. (2003) 'Prior juvenile diagnoses in adults with mental disorder'. *Archives of General Psychiatry*, Vol. 60, p709-717.

archpsyc.ama-assn.org/cgi/content/abstract/60/7/709

Lepper, J. (2011) Mental Health Early Intervention Projects offer Outstanding Value. www.cypnow.co.uk/News/EmailIt/1066599/C9B931880E06400CCE10CEE8920918B1/

MacConville, R. (2008) *Teaching Happiness*. London: Optimus Education.

Mental Health First Aid England (2010) www.mhfaengland.org

Mental Health Foundation (2006) *Truth Hurts: Report of the National Inquiry into Self-Harm Among Young People*. London: Mental Health Foundation.

www.mentalhealth.org.uk/content/assets/PDF/.../truth_hurts.pdf

Mental Health Foundation (2011)

www.mentalhealth.org.uk/

Mental Health Policy Group (2006)

cep.lse.ac.uk/_new/research/mentalhealth/default.asp

Meltzer, H., Lader, D. & Corbin, T. (2002) *Non-Fatal Suicidal Behaviour Among Adults aged 16 to 74 in Great Britain*. London: The Stationary Office.

Meltzer, H., Gatward, R., Corbin, T. et al. (2003) *The Mental Health of Young People Looked After by Local Authorities in England*. London: Stationery Office.

www.dh.gov.uk/en/Publicationsandstatistics/Publications/PublicationsStatistics/DH_4019442

Mitchell, R. (2009) *Wake Up Shake Up*, Cornwall.
www.lostwithiel.cornwall.sch.uk/2011/11/p-e-wake-up-shake-up/

National Health Service (2011) *Improving Access to Psychological Therapies*. www.iapt.nhs.uk/

National Institute for Health and Clinical Excellence (2012) www.nice.org.uk

National Society for the Prevention of Cruelty to Children (2009)
www.nspcc.org.uk

New Economics Foundation (2004) *A Wellbeing Manifesto for a Flourishing Society.*
www.neweconomics.org/publications/wellbeing-manifesto-flourishing-society

New Economics Foundation (2008) The Foresight Programme Mental Capital and Wellbeing Project.

www.neweconomics.org

Nicholls, D. (2011) 'Eating Disorders in Adolescence'. *In Child Psychology and Psychiatry: Frameworks for Practice, Second Edition.* University College London: Institute of Child Health.

http://onlinelibrary.wiley.com/doi/10.1002/9781119993971.ch31/summary

Office for Public Management (2010) *Evaluation of Healthy Minds Matter. Final Report to Gloucestershire Primary Care Trust.*

www.opm.co.uk

Office for National Statistics (1997) Psychiatric morbidity among young offenders in England and Wales. London: Office for National Statistics.

www.dh.gov.uk/en/Publicationsandstatistics/Publications/PublicationsStatistics/DH_4009274

Office for National Statistics (2004) Census 2001: *National Report for England and Wales.* London: Office for National Statistics.

www.ons.gov.uk/ons/guide-method/census/2011/index.html

Palmer, S. (2007) *Detoxing Childhood.* London: Orion Publishing.

www.orionbooks.co.uk

Pearce, B. (2003) Modelling the Role of Infections in the Etiology of Mental Illness [online].

www.sciencedirect.com/science/article/pii/S1566277203000987

Place2be (2011) [online]

www.theplace2be.org.uk

Samaritans (2011) [online]
www.samaritans.org.uk

Sawyer, M. G., Arney, F. M., Baghurst, P. A., Clark, J. J., Graetz, B. W., Kosky, R. J., Nurcombe, B., Patton, G. C., Prior, M. R., Raphael, B., Rey, J., Whaites, L. C. & Zubrick, S. R. (2000) Child and Adolescent Component of the National Survey of Mental Health and Wellbeing.

www.quitnow.gov.au/Internet/main/publishing.nsf/Content/70DA14F816CC7A8FCA257 28800104564/$File/young.pdf

Seligman, M. (1998) *Authentic Happiness*. Boston: Nicholas Brealey Publishing. www. authentichappiness.sas.upenn.edu/Default.aspx

Strauch, B. (2003) *Why are they so Weird? What's really going on in a Teenager's Brain*. London: Bloomsbury Publishing PLC.

The Children and Young People's Mental Health Coalition (2010) Improving Children and Young People's Mental Health.
www.cypmhc.org.uk/resources/improving_children_and_young_peoples_mental_health/

Thompson, P. (2006) Royal College of Psychiatrists: London.
www.repsych.ac.uk

The World Health Organisation and International Early Psychosis Organisation (2004)
www.iris-initiative.org.uk

Unicef (2007) *Child Poverty in Perspective – An Overview of Child Wellbeing in Rich Countries*. Italy: Innocenti Report.

Ward, S. (2008) *Understanding Concepts for Working with Children and Young People*. Belfast: Health Promotion Agency.
www.healthpromotionagency.org.uk

Weare, K. (2004) *Developing the Emotionally Literate School*. London: Paul Chapman Publishing.

Wilson, P. (2004) *Young Minds in Our Schools*.
www.youngminds.org.uk

World Health Organisation (2001) The World Health Report, Geneva.
www.who.int

World Health Organisation (2007)
www.who.int/entity/maternal_child_adolescent/topics/adolescence/mental_health/en/

2gether NHS Foundation Trust for Gloucestershire (2004) The Little Book of Mental Health.

www.pmhsglos.org.uk

Young Minds (2006)
www.youngminds.org.uk